Tipping The Balance

The Mental Skills Handbook For Athletes

Dr Martin Turner

Dr Jamie Barker

BENNION
KEARNY

D1581791

Published in 2014 by Bennion Kearny Limited.

Copyright © Bennion Kearny Ltd 2014

Martin Turner and Jamie Barker have asserted their rights under the Copyright, Designs and Patents Act, 1988 to be identified as the authors of this book.

Technical Editor: Dr Charlotte Woodcock

ISBN: 978-1-909125-93-3

Published by Bennion Kearny Limited
6 Woodside
Churnet View Road
Oakamoor
ST10 3AE

www.BennionKearny.com

For Jayne, always and forever.

Martin

For Emma, Lucy, Molly and the rest of my family,
for all your love and support

Jamie

For Professor Marc Jones, whose thoughts and ideas
have inspired both of us and much of this book.

Both

Acknowledgements

Martin Turner: This book, and indeed my career to date, would not exist without the occurrence of some highly significant events, and without the influence of some highly significant people. I thank Professor Marc Jones, whose influence on my career is immeasurable. Many of our conversations about the psychology of performance (and some of our research!) made it into this book in some way or another. I also thank my co-author, colleague, and friend, Associate Professor Jamie Barker, who saw something in me when I was an undergraduate that I didn't know was there; a passion for psychology. In some ways this book has existed in my head for some time, but my gratitude goes out to our editor and publisher James for bringing those thoughts and ideas to life. I thank all of the athletes and coaches I have worked with, and continue to work with, to date. I gain a huge amount from the work we have done, and continue to do together. In addition, I thank all of the colleagues that have supported me in my research and consultancy to date, you know who you are.

Jayne, when I met you I was directionless and inert. You gave me purpose and energy. Thank you for being there and for being you. As with all that I do, this book is for you.

Jamie Barker: This book is the culmination of many years of research and applied practice and would not exist without the influence of a number of key individuals. I would like to express my sincere thanks to my friend, colleague and co-author, Dr Martin Turner. Martin is an excellent academic with a very bright future. I thank him for continuing to support and challenge my thinking along with keeping my beliefs rational. I also thank Professor Marc Jones who continues to provide excellent mentorship in helping me to shape my ideas and goals. I would also like to thank all of my colleagues who have supported my research and applied work - it is a pleasure working with such talented and creative individuals.

I am indebted to my parents, Linda and Roger, for giving me the confidence to have 'no regrets' and for their continued love and support in everything I do. I owe everything to the endless patience, support and love of my wife Emma - you are a truly remarkable wife and mother. Finally, to my daughters, Lucy and Molly - you are my world and all I am I give to you - just not the season ticket!

About the Authors

Dr Martin Turner is a Lecturer in Sport and Exercise Psychology in the School of Psychology, Sport and Exercise at Staffordshire University. Martin is an active researcher and a Chartered practitioner psychologist. He consults with professional athletes, teams, and coaches, and also works with business professionals and management in multinational organizations.

Dr Jamie Barker is Associate Professor of Applied Performance Psychology at Staffordshire University, and a Chartered psychologist. Jamie is an active researcher and contributor to the Centre for Sport, Health, and Exercise Research (CSHER), works with athletes, coaches and sports teams across many disciplines, and is the co-author of the acclaimed Bennion Kearny title: *The Psychology of Cricket: Developing Mental Toughness*, amongst others.

Contents

The Performance

The crowd erupts. It's deafening. It's enough to turn my stomach.

That felt good. I return to my chair after my warm-up to rapturous applause and cheers that shake the arena and fill me with energy. My warm-up was a great reminder of how hard I have worked in the lead-up to this match. I feel rested and fresh. My diet, my commitment in training, my unstoppable quest to improve every single day. I am a well-oiled and perfectly fuelled machine that is peaking at the right moment. All of the things that are in my control have been meticulously controlled. I don't know how my competitor will perform. I cannot control this aspect of the match so I will focus on *what I can control*; my performance. Today is about doing what I do best, which is playing excellent solid tennis, and being a professional.

I sit alone in my chair, in the arena, looking out onto the court. This is the biggest match of my career, and the first time my country has reached the tournament final in its history. This burden weighs heavy, but this is my chance to fulfil my potential. One chance to make history. Family, friends, and supporters look on in anxious and desperate hope that I succeed today. I want to win more than anything in the world, and losing would be the biggest disappointment of my career.

In my chair, I start to exercise control over my performance preparations. I go into my systematic mental routine, the same routine I use for each match, to ensure that I am in the right state to fulfil my potential. I am now inside my mind. Although my eyes are open I am processing nothing external to my body and mind.

A quick body scan reveals that I am nervous. Shaking legs, queasiness, and a racing heart tell me that my body is doing what it can to prepare me for the intensely physical battle that I am about to encounter. I picture the blood rushing to my brain and limbs, carrying with it the oxygen and energy I will require to produce a performance here. I am lucky that my body does this naturally, helping me to prepare for performance. I focus on my breathing for a moment, turning a heavy and confused pattern into a rhythmic and controlled pulse. I feel composed now.

1

The Performance

Feeling like a machine on standby, I watch a movie in my head. The film is about me and it's an epic. It contains footage from the future and I see 'me' expressing myself fully on court: perfect ground strokes, precision serves, high energy, controlling the tempo, getting to every ball. As I picture this epic, I can feel the impact of each stroke in my arms and hands; I hear the ball leave my racket and echo around the arena, and I can smell the sweat from my shirt breeze past my face as I move swiftly back into position. I create all of this in my head. I see everything through my own eyes and it's a picture of dominance and laser-like focus on each point. Everything I do, I know I can do, and have done before.

Year after year, match after match, the pressure of performing has shaped who I am and has toughened me. What was once trepidation is now excitement. I can't wait to get this match started so I can show people what I am capable of.

As I snap out of this positive bubble, I remind myself of my key jobs today: "express myself fully", "control the tempo", and "make every shot count". As I say these words in my head, the images return like a highlight reel from my future.

It's getting close now. My body is ready, my mind is ready. It's my service game that will start the match. I focus only on the things I need to do to perform well. I remind myself to "serve aggressively", "set myself after each serve", and "stay on my toes for a possible return". I see myself executing these elements perfectly in my head, over and over again. This is all I have in my mind, nothing else matters at this moment.

The umpire signals and I stand to take to the court. I trigger my laser-like focus by reminding myself that "I am ready". I walk with chest out, back straight, shoulders back: the picture of confidence.

The crowd quietens as I stare straight down at the baseline I stand upon. As I bounce the ball I visualize my serve. In my mind I see the ball in my hand and I toss it to the perfect height above my stretched body. As I swing through the ball I feel my muscles jolt with power. The ball disappears over the net… then blank.

As my mind clears I toss the ball upwards. Now it's time for my mind and body to take charge.

It's time for the big show. It's time to perform.

A Winning State of Body and Mind

How are the best athletes in the world able to function under the immense pressure of competitive performance? By harnessing the potential of their minds to stay committed, train smart, and get themselves into a winning state of body and mind when the time is right.

This book is about getting *you* into a winning state of body and mind for your sporting performances. The ability of elite athletes to exercise control over their mental and physical states during performance can offer many lessons to anyone who wants to fulfil their potential when it matters most.

The example, above, contained many of the key elements to accessing the winning mindset. This book will help you to develop your own way, just like the tennis athlete developed his own way. We hope you are ready for a journey that will maximize you and your potential. Enjoy the ride!

Chapter 1: γνῶθι σεαυτόν (Know Thyself)

 Nervousness took over first his mind, and then his body... The contrast between the commanding McIlroy of day three and the disconsolate McIlroy of day four came down to psychology – no more and no less. Between the first and the third day, he had convinced himself he could win; by the fourth, he feared he could not.[1]

Brian Viner, Journalist and Author

The above quote neatly captures the essence of this first chapter. The mind and body are inextricably linked so that if the functioning of the mind is erroneous, so too is our physical performance.

The quote relates to Rory McIlroy, professional golfer, World Number One, and a four-time major champion; a man who experienced one of the most catastrophic and highly public performance meltdowns of recent times. At the 2011 Masters, on the final day, McIlroy was leading the field when he got to the 10th hole. At the 10th, something went wrong very suddenly, and very badly.

McIlroy pulled his drive into the trees, and the ball ended up nestling next to the white wooden cabins alongside the fairway, 100 yards from the tee. McIlroy laudably chipped out of an awkward position for his second shot, but then pulled his third. His fourth shot was a chip from under the green that rolled back towards him once it had landed. McIlroy eventually chipped onto the green and putted the ball in two, scoring seven in total. He dropped from first place to seventh on one hole, never to regain his form from earlier in the round. On the 11th he missed a putt from about 30 inches, which is highly irregular. "I was still one shot ahead going into the 10th and then things went all pear-shaped after that," McIlroy said at the time.[2]

We shouldn't feel too bad for Rory McIlroy though - he came back to win the next Major, proving quite unequivocally how our reactions to pressure can be altered, and how stressful experiences can help us to overcome future adversity (more about this in chapter 9).

I don't know if I had not had that day, whether I would be the person and the player I am sitting here. I learned exactly what not to do under pressure and in contention and definitely learned how to handle my emotions better on the course.[3]

Rory McIlroy, Golfer

So, to kick off, let's explore the mind-body connection, and explain what McIlroy (and anyone else who has choked when it mattered most) experienced that so effectively destroyed his performance.

Importantly, and reassuringly, our reactions to pressure situations can be altered.

What Happens to the Mind Under Pressure?

Let's begin our exploration into what happens to the mind and body when under pressure by conducting a quick thought experiment.

Task 1

Imagine that you are poised at the start of a tightrope walk, standing on a platform looking down at the rope pulled securely between your platform and another platform ten feet away. The tightrope is suspended one foot off the ground. Your task is to walk along the tightrope to get to the finish platform. Visualize yourself in this situation. Close your eyes if it helps. How does your body feel? What thoughts do you have? What are your chances of success? What are the consequences of failure? How important is success in this task?

Task 2

Now, once again imagine that you are poised at the start of a tightrope walk, standing on a platform looking down at the rope pulled securely between your platform and a platform ten feet away. But this time, the tightrope is suspended *ten* feet off the ground. Your task is to walk along the tightrope to get to the finish platform. Again, really try to see yourself in this situation, eyes closed if that helps. How does your body feel? What thoughts do you have? What are your chances of success? What are the consequences of failure? How important is success in this task?

Your answers to the questions for the two tasks probably differ markedly. If you were actually to perform the tasks, your reactions to each situation would be like comparing apples to oranges. Perhaps for task 1 your thoughts reflected the desire to get across the rope to the other side as efficiently as possible. Maybe there were some doubts about your ability to do this, but largely you felt that it was a challenge you could meet.

In contrast, perhaps your thoughts for task 2 reflected a need to simply 'get across' the rope as failure would mean significant injury. And maybe you focused on that fear of falling and the pain you may experience if you fail, so much so, that you harboured wishes to avoid the task altogether. This is important and interesting for two main reasons.

First, the tasks are exactly the same with regard to the physical demands placed on you. You only have to walk ten feet in both tasks, across the same rope. The only difference is that task 1 is performed one foot off the ground, and task 2 - ten feet off the ground.

Second, in task 2, you need to feel composed, confident, and focused on success, because failure may result in serious injury. Ironically this is precisely when composure eludes us, confidence escapes us, and our focus fixes on potential failure. The added physical danger of task 2 alters our perception of the task so drastically, that we can fail to realize that the task has the same physical requirements. Instead, the importance of performing well and avoiding the negative consequences of failure (serious injury) becomes our main focus.

In short, it is not the requirements of the task itself that create pressure; it is our perceptions of those requirements that create the pressure. Further, if we asked you to perform the two tasks but this time, in front of an audience, or offered a lucrative prize for success, again the tasks would be the same, but greater perceptions of pressure would be induced.

People often talk about "pressure situations" and "being put under pressure". But, in sport, pressure is an internal phenomenon. That is, pressure comes from within, not without.

---

*It is not the task that creates pressure,
it's our perceptions.*

In sport, the penalty shoot-out in football illustrates the above point nicely. Imagine you are an elite soccer player and after a 90-minute closely fought match against your rivals in the cup, the game is tied and extra time is played. However, a stalemate ensues and a penalty shoot-out will decide the contest.

Let's have a go at another thought experiment.

Task 1

Imagine your team are winning the shoot-out 4-3, and you have been selected by the manager to take the fifth penalty for your team. If you score, you win. If you don't score, the opposition may equalise thus taking the shoot-out to sudden death. Reflect on how you would approach this kick. How does your body feel? What thoughts do you have? What are your chances of success? What are the consequences of failure? How important is success in this task?

Task 2

Now imagine your team are *losing* the shoot-out 5-4, and you have been selected by the manager to take the fifth penalty for your team. If you score, you equalise and make it 5-5, and the shoot-out goes to sudden death. If you don't score, your team lose, and you are the one who sealed their fate. Reflect on how you would approach this kick. How does your body feel? What thoughts do you have? What are your chances of success? What are the consequences of failure? How important is success in this task?

Your reflections of how you would feel going into these penalty kicks are again based not on the task itself (both require you to score a penalty against the same goal keeper), but on the gravity of the situation and the consequences of your kick. If you score in task 1, you are the hero – you win the match for your team. If you miss, there is still a chance for your team to win. The potential gains are more salient than the potential losses. If you score in task 2, you have done your job but there is still a chance that your team could lose. If you miss, you are the villain as you have knocked your team out of the cup. The potential losses are more significant than the potential gains. Typically, when faced with a difficult task where the potential losses are particularly relevant (and are used as motivation), perceived pressure is inflated and performance will, in most situations, suffer.

Something similar to the above happened recently when Brazil played Chile in the second round of the 2014 World Cup. Picture the scene; after four penalty kicks each, the score was tied at Chile 2 Brazil 2. Neymar, poster boy for the World Cup, starts his lonely walk towards the penalty spot from the centre of the field. He is taking the last penalty for Brazil, which will decide whether his team, the home nation, will progress to the next round. With the world watching his every move, and knowing that one kick will decide his and his country's fate, he stands over the ball. The referee signals for him to take the kick. He approaches the ball, shuffles his feet, and calmly slots the ball into the net like it's the easiest thing in the world. Jara, who steps up to take Chile's last penalty knows that if he misses, his team are out. He takes a quick run-up to get this ordeal over with, and sends a rocket towards goal. He hits the post. He misses. Chile are out, Brazil stay in. One highly pressured situation, two very different outcomes.

A penalty kick is a relatively easy skill for all professional soccer players, and the odds are stacked in the penalty taker's favour. In training, the athlete can quite easily score a penalty. But add the meaningfulness of a cup final, or the gravity of a World Cup, and some of the best players in the world can produce uncoordinated and uncharacteristically poor penalties. The task is the same as they would have practiced in training; it is the importance of the situation that is different, and the apparent consequences of failure. Indeed, current England soccer manager Roy Hodgson highlights how the perceived importance of the occasion can influence performance: "You can practise penalty shoot-outs until the cows come home but it's really all about composure, confidence and an ability to block everything out and forget the occasion."[4]

The team which handles the pressure best, carries the day.[5]

Imran Khan, Cricketer

So it is our perceptions of events that cause pressure; the importance, the gravity, the consequences of failure. Take these factors away and most 'stressful' situations would become rather tame encounters.

Take a Look in the Mirror

The tasks you have completed so far in this chapter have encouraged you to be aware of your thoughts and feelings prior to performance (or imagined performance) under pressure. Being able to reflect on how you think and feel under pressure is a vital step towards explaining why you may have underperformed in the past.

It is also a vital step towards identifying what skills you need to work on to make sure underperformance does not happen again. This chapter is called "Know Thyself" - taken from Dan Goleman's highly influential book "Emotional Intelligence: Why It Can Matter More Than IQ".[6] In it, Goleman describes self-awareness as the building block of self-control. Not only will an awareness of what happens to the mind and body under pressure help to demystify why you sometimes thrive and why (at other times) you fail when it matters most, it will also move you towards being able to control and take charge of your mind and body under pressure. You can use the following table to consider what your thoughts and feelings were before and during successful and unsuccessful performances.

My *successful* performances	My thoughts and feelings before, and during, my successful performances
My *unsuccessful* performances	My thoughts and feelings before, and during, my unsuccessful performances

What Happens to the Body Under Pressure?

The mind and the body are inextricably linked, and there is no greater evidence for this fact than our ability to imagine and recreate events in our minds, causing bodily changes that reflect the imagined situation.

You can illustrate this easily by using a heart rate monitor (free and widely available these days using smart phone Apps). Get nice and relaxed, and look at the heart rate reading. Make a note of it. Now think back to a time when you were under immense pressure in your sport. Take a moment to dwell on this situation for a minute or so. Now check your heart rate reading! Typically, there will be a significant increase in heart rate (more about this in chapter 8).

Alternatively, look forward to an upcoming high pressure competition you are facing. Most probably, your heart rate is higher when thinking about the situation compared to when you were completely relaxed.

The body's reactions to pressure are not limited to the heart. Most professional athletes will talk about experiencing a vast, and highly individualized, array of physical feelings when they perceive a pressure situation. These often include stomach butterflies, sweaty palms, tense muscles, nausea, and lethargy (or sometimes, in contrast, hyperactivity and restlessness). David Hemery, prior to his World Record in the 1968 Olympic Games, recalled: "Standing behind my blocks, I put my hands on my knees and tried to take as deep a breath as I could. I could not completely fill my lungs... My mouth and throat were dry, it was impossible to swallow. I wished I could be anywhere else."[7]

The brain rapidly evaluates the nature of the situation and organizes the body's responses accordingly.

This next point is very important to our understanding of bodily responses to pressure: *these physical symptoms are normal and are designed to help us out.*

The symptoms are all part of what is known as the 'stress response', or commonly "fight or flight"[8] mode, which occurs in demanding situations where success has positive consequences for our careers or lives, and where failure has negative consequences. When faced with such a situation, the brain very quickly evaluates the personal meaning of success and failure and then rapidly organizes our physiological reactions.

The stress response has been programmed through generation upon generation of evolution to make sure we can respond quickly to dangers to our survival. Joseph LeDoux, neuroscientist and author of the acclaimed book "The Emotional Brain"[9] describes this evolutionary point excellently, on The LeDoux Lab website, explaining that...

Chapter 1

"…early on (perhaps since dinosaurs ruled the earth, or even before) evolution hit upon a way of wiring the brain to produce responses that are likely to keep the organism alive in dangerous situations. The solution was so effective that it has not been messed with much… Evolution seems to have gone with an "if it ain't broke, don't fix it" rule when it comes to the fear system of the brain."[10]

So, our biology has not developed as quickly as our living circumstances, and we have been left with a fear response that is triggered by (comparatively) minor challenges. That is, instead of having to escape or kill a sabre-toothed tiger, we now have to compete for medals and trophies, and be evaluated and judged by coaches, scouts and spectators!

Because the stress response happens so quickly, it occurs unconsciously and automatically - based on our initial rapid evaluation of the situation. The good news is, the response is helpful because the heart beats faster, sending important chemicals such as glucose and adrenaline to the parts of the body required for sport performance in a given task. This cardiovascular reaction is crucial for sport performance; it allows for the rapid delivery of oxygen and energy to the muscles and the brain – this allows you to perform physically and also to make key decisions. This surge, often called the adrenaline rush, is responsible for the physical symptoms you may experience before a competition or important trial (e.g., sweaty palms, muscle tension, racing heart).

So far, so good. Many of you may have read similar descriptions before, and many of you may have gained some genuine insight into your body's responses to pressure. The idea that we can respond quickly to help service the muscles and brain for sport performance is reassuring but there is one important piece of information we need to share with you; it helps form one of the key aspects of this book. There are two separate ways that we can respond to pressure; *one good for performance, and one bad.*

These two responses have been called *challenge* and *threat* states[11], and research shows that when approaching pressure situations, athletes experiencing a challenge state perform well (better than normal, in fact), and when they experience a threat state they perform poorly (worse than normal). This is evidenced across various sports with both elite and non-elite athletes.[12] [13] [14] [15]

In our own research, with elite cricketers, we have found that athletes who respond to a pressured batting test in a challenge state perform better (they scored more runs and were dismissed less often) when compared to those who respond in a threat state. But what does this challenge state actually consist of? How does it differ from a threat state?

Challenge state helps performance.
Threat state hinders performance.

A challenge state reflects a positive mental approach to pressure situations where our mental resources meet the demands of the situation (more about this in the next chapter). The body reacts to this mental approach with increased heart rate, an increase in the amount of blood pumped from the heart per minute, and a decrease in vascular (blood vessels) constriction, from normal resting levels. Blood is delivered to the brain efficiently, and this is highly important for mental functions such as concentration, decision making, and having control over thoughts and emotions. It is also important for the delivery of energy and oxygen to muscles, for short and long-term physical movement and skill execution. If you think back to times when you have succeeded in your sport, your performance was most probably preceded by thoughts and feelings of positivity and confidence.

A threat state reflects a negative mental approach to pressure situations where our mental resources do not meet the demands of the situation (again, more about this in the next chapter). The body reacts to this mental approach with an increased heart rate (as in a challenge state), but this time with a decrease or stabilization in the amount of blood pumped from the heart per minute, and an increase in vascular (blood vessels) constriction, from normal resting levels. In other words, the amount of blood pumped from the heart is largely unchanged. This means that the delivery of glucose and oxygen to the brain and muscles is inefficient, not helping you to perform at your best when it matters most. The brain and muscles need glucose and oxygen to function properly (e.g., make effective decisions, perform physically), so the more efficiently you can deliver these substances to the brain and muscles, the better you will be able to perform mentally (e.g., make decisions) and physically (e.g., execute skills). Indeed, reflecting back on times when you have not succeeded in your sport may reveal that prior to your performance you felt worried and uncertain.

Challenge State

Threat State

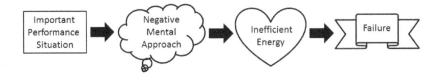

The principles of challenge and threat have huge implications for your sport performance. By approaching a competition in the right mental state you can harness the body's natural ability to energize your brain to make accurate decisions and think clearly, and the muscles to execute complex and intricate skills when it really counts. In short, the right mental approach leads to a challenge state, helping you to fulfil your potential.

Brief Summary

How aware are you of your responses to pressure? Can you reflect on how your body feels? Can you access your thoughts? Do you know how your feelings and thoughts affect your sport performance?

This first chapter has expressed the importance of self-awareness. We have clarified how the mind and body interact in pressure situations and have introduced you to the notion that pressure is about perception first and foremost. It is the gravity and importance of the situation and the consequences of failure that determines your experience of pressure. But secondly and more importantly, we have introduced the notion that you can respond to pressure in a good way (a challenge state) and a bad way (a threat state), which has implications for how the mind and body react to pressure and ultimately how you perform in your sport.

The idea that we can respond in two different ways to pressure, one good for performance and one bad, is at the core of this book. To explain, if you are able to get yourself into a challenge state for pressured sport performances like competitions and trials, and help others to do the same, you can get the best out of yourself and others when it counts.

The rest of this book is about how you can develop mental skills to enhance challenge states.

Most Important Point

Because your reaction to pressure, and subsequent performance success, depends on your perceptions of the situation and yourself, modifying your perceptions to be more helpful for performance is the key to fulfilling your potential.

Chapter 1

The Next Chapter is Vital

Knowing how and why your brain and body reacts under pressure is important. But as Morpheus in the blockbuster film "The Matrix" said: "There is a difference between knowing the path and walking the path"[16]

The next chapter introduces The MAPP (Map to Achieving Peak Performance), which will facilitate "knowing the path". Subsequent chapters will then teach you how to "walk the path". Specifically, the next chapter moves on to explain how you can get into a challenge state and details an easy-to-follow 'MAPP for Success', which outlines the many determinants of a challenge state.

A bit of structure is useful here - The MAPP will help you to understand where gaps in your mental skills toolkit might be, and consequently which of the chapters in this book might be of most use to you.

By learning the techniques in this book you will arrive at the ultimate goal: the ability to respond adaptively in tough situations in your sport, getting yourself and others into a challenge state when it matters most, and subsequently performing to the best of your abilities!

---

[1] Viner, B. (2011, April 12). Beyond a choke: what becomes of the sporting imploder? *The Independent*, p. 12.

[2] Murrells, K. (2011, April 11). Masters 2011: I'll get over Augusta disappointment, says Rory McIlroy. *The Guardian*. Retrieved May 21, 2014, from http://www.theguardian.com/sport/2011/apr/11/masters-2011-rory-mcilroy-schwartzel

[3] Hodgetts, R. (2014, April 8). Masters 2014: Rory McIlroy unfazed by Augusta meltdown. *BBC*. Retrieved May 21, 2014, from http://www.bbc.co.uk/sport/0/golf/26948243

[4] Winter, H. (2014, May 13). World Cup 2014: England reject chance to practise penalty shoot-out in public. *The Telegraph*. Retrieved May 21, 2014, from http://www.telegraph.co.uk/sport/football/teams/england/10829014/Wo

rld-Cup-2014-England-reject-chance-to-practise-penalty-shoot-out-in-pubilc.html

[5] The team which handles the pressure best, carries the day (n. d.). *In searchquotes.com*. Retrieved May 21, 2014, from http://www.cns.nyu.edu/labs/ledouxlab/overview.htm

[6] Goleman, D. (1995). *Emotional Intelligence: Why it Can Matter More Than IQ*. London: Bloomsbury Publishing plc.

[7] Hemery, D. (2012, June 12). David Hemery: 'I didn't know I had won, let alone beaten the world record'. *The Independent*. Retrieved May 21, 2014, from http://www.independent.co.uk/sport/olympics/david-hemery-i-didnt-know-i-had-won-let-alone-beaten-the-world-record-7836933.html

[8] Cannon, W. B. (1939). *The wisdom of the body* (2nd edition.). New York: W. W. Norton.

[9] Ledoux, J. (1998). *The emotional brain*. New York: Simon & Schuster.

[10] Emotion, memory & the brain. (n.d.). *In The LeDoux Lab*. Retrieved May 21, 2014, from http://www.cns.nyu.edu/labs/ledouxlab/overview.htm

[11] Blascovich, J., & Mendes, W. B. (2000). Challenge and threat appraisals: the role of affective cues. In J. P. Forgas (Ed.) *Feeling and thinking: the role of affect in social cognition* (pp. 59-82). Paris: Cambridge University Press.

[12] Blascovich, J., Seery, M. D., Mugridge, C. A., Norris, R. K., & Weisbuch, M. (2004). Predicting athletic performance from cardiovascular indexes of challenge and threat. *Journal of Experimental Social Psychology*, 40, 683-688.

[13] Moore, L. J., Vine, S. J., Wilson, M. R., & Freeman, P. (2012). The effect of challenge and threat states on performance: An examination of potential mechanisms. *Psychophysiology*, 49, (10), 1417-1425. doi: 10.1111/j.1469-8986.2012.01449.x

[14] Turner, M. J., Jones, M. V., Sheffield, D., & Cross, S. L. (2012). Cardiovascular indices of challenge and threat states predict performance under stress in cognitive and motor tasks. International *Journal of Psychophysiology*, 86, (1), 48-57. doi:10.1016/j.ijpsycho.2012.08.004

[15] Turner, M. J., Jones, M. V., Sheffield, D., Slater, M. J., Barker, J. B., & Bell, J. (2013). Who thrives under pressure? Predicting the performance of elite academy cricketers using the cardiovascular indicators of challenge and threat states. *Journal of Sport and Exercise Psychology*, 35, (4), 387-397.

[16] Quotes for Morpheus. (n.d.). *In IMDb*. Retrieved May 21, 2014, from http://www.imdb.com/character/ch0000746/quotes

Chapter 2: Be Challenged

 Everything negative - pressure, challenges - is all an opportunity for me to rise.[1]

Kobe Bryant, Basketball Player

How can we end up like Kobe Bryant? Seeing important situations - where the pressure is high - as a challenge to be overcome is something elite athletes talk about a lot. But this isn't just something you can or cannot do; it's a skill to be learned. That is, your reactions to pressure are not fixed; they can be developed and honed. Kobe Bryant clearly thrives under pressure, while others merely survive.

There is a big difference between surviving under pressure and thriving. As the late Maya Angelou, American poet and American Civil Rights activist, proclaimed: "Surviving is important. Thriving is elegant."[2]

You can *learn* to thrive, and one of the important lessons of this book is that you can face pressure positively, without trying to convince yourself that your performance isn't important. Many athletes we have worked with try to convince themselves that key performances are actually not that important, as a way to deal with the pressure. But, of course, that end of season cup final or Olympic final is crucial for you and your career. Pretending that these crucial performances are not important is both unrealistic and pointless. Remember, pressure is not 'bad', and situation importance does not create negative reactions to pressure. It's your mental approach to that important situation that counts.

If you change the way you mentally approach performance, you change your reaction to the situation. The tennis player Andy Murray, insightfully, has it right when analysing pressure: "The only pressure I feel is the pressure I put on myself to win."[3] Similarly, Paula Radcliffe, current World Record holder for the women's marathon, has made clear that: "The biggest pressure comes from within you."[4]

So stop thinking about pressure as something that is put on you!

Chapter 2 - Be Challenged - is about learning to see important situations as a challenge to be overcome, and recognizing that no matter how important a situation is, you are the master of your reactions to it.

Chapter 1 encouraged you to be aware of what happens in the mind and body when you compete. We arrived at the notion that, in important situations, we can respond in two different ways, one good for performance (a challenge state) and one bad (a threat state). As a consequence, having the ability to get yourself into a challenge state for important sport performance situations and also helping others to do the same, is crucial for achieving peak performance.

Luckily, there is a 'MAPP for Success' that provides a guide to what causes challenge and threat states. Fundamentally, The MAPP tells you how to get yourself into a challenge state. Once you have learned what it takes to get into a challenge state, you can digest the subsequent chapters and make things happen at the coalface.

The MAPP is a guide to what causes challenge and threat states, so that you can understand what you can do to get yourself into a challenge state.

The rest of this chapter guides you through the MAPP and will serve as a useful reference point for the remainder of the book. Most importantly, this chapter will help you to understand that the first step to achieving peak performance - when it matters most - is to see the situation as a challenge to be *overcome*, rather than a threat to be *avoided*. Let's get stuck in!

Explaining The MAPP

The MAPP is based on decades of work by sport psychologists all over the world, but is mainly based on The Theory of Challenge and Threat States in Athletes developed by Professor Marc Jones, Dr. Carla Meijen, Dr. Paul McCarthy, and Professor David Sheffield.[5]

The first thing you will notice is that The MAPP is a step-by-step process. It begins with the performance situation you are faced with. This might be a trial, a penalty shoot-out, the final round of a golf tournament, an Olympic final, or one of many other performance situations you may face within your sport.

The second step concerns your philosophy surrounding success and failure. For you, maybe success is a 'must', and failure is 'terrible', or in contrast perhaps success is preferable, and failure is bad but not terrible (more of this in chapter 3).

In the third step the demands of the situation are processed, and this involves an evaluation of the uncertainty, required effort, and danger (both physical and to esteem) present in the performance situation.

The fourth step, on which we will focus much of our attention, comprises of an evaluation into the resources available to you in the situation and is made up of three crucial factors: self-confidence, control, and achievement goals.

Chapter 2

The MAPP for Success

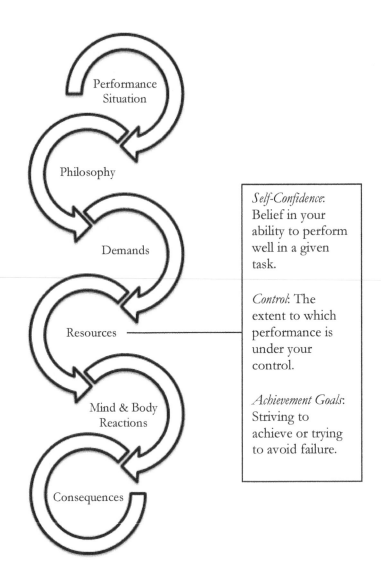

These initial four steps are the vital precursors of challenge and threat states. If the sport situation is not deemed important to you, neither challenge nor threat will occur, because the situation simply isn't meaningful enough to be perceived as pressured.

Assuming the sport performance situation is important to us, and if our philosophy includes an overemphasis on the severity of failure, our evaluation of demands will be distorted. In the most important performance situations our evaluations include an uncertain outcome (few outcomes are certain), a requirement for effort (success in sport usually does not come easily), and some danger to our esteem (if I fail, I - or others - will think less of me).

But here is an important part of the initial four steps: *if the resources meet the demands, a challenge state will occur.*

Equally as importantly: *if the resources do not meet the demands, a threat state will occur.*

You could think of this like a set of weighing scales, where our resources are weighed against demands. Our goal in this calculation is to outweigh the demands with our resources, so that the scales tip in our favour for performance.

So, the most obvious strategy for getting into a challenge state is to enhance your resources; in particular, to increase your ability to feel confident, be in control, and remain focused on what *can* be achieved instead of what can be lost. In other words, develop your own challenge strategy to help you wield resources that outweigh the demands of any sport performance situation.

A challenge state helps you to fulfil your potential.

Chris Hoy and His First Olympic Gold Medal

Let's look at an example of how The MAPP might work in a real life sport competition. Let's choose a high profile elite athlete… Chris Hoy, the most decorated Olympic cyclist of all time.

There is nothing quite like an Olympic story to assess the demands of resources in a real-life sport situation. One of the most amazing events in the last decade was Chris Hoy's first Gold Medal in Athens in 2004. The event was the 1k time trial, which simply means that the athlete has to go as quickly as possible around the track for a distance of 1 kilometre. As reigning world champion in this event, Hoy was to go last in this time trial. As Hoy waited for his trial, his competitors clocked quicker and quicker times. One after another, the Olympic record fell, until the Frenchman Arnaud Tournant, who raced directly before Hoy, clocked in at 1:00.896 – another record!

So to win gold in the 1K, Hoy had to go faster than he had ever gone before, and faster than any man had ever gone before at sea level.

The result? Hoy powered round the track in a time of 1:00.711, the fastest time ever at sea level.

Obviously, this race was highly important for Hoy (step 1 in The MAPP), and we cannot know what his philosophy around success and failure (step 2 in The MAPP) may have been. But we can analyse Hoy's potential demands (step 3 in The MAPP) and resources (step 4 in The MAPP) to try to understand how Hoy managed to prevail amidst great pressure.

First, the Demands

Uncertainty

Even though Hoy was the world champion in this event, the Olympic Gold was by no means his for the taking. Athletes at Hoy's level deliberately peak at the Olympics. Their training and competitive season leads up to the Olympics so that, when they are at the starting line, they are in top shape and can bring out their best performance for the Olympics. So, although Hoy was the favourite, the result was still highly uncertain. Hoy recalls, "It was just the first time that you do something of that magnitude,...To become Olympic champion for the first time whether you're the favourite or not, whether you've beaten everyone in the field before, it means nothing until you've actually done it on the night, when it counts."[6]

This is one of the things that makes the Olympics so stressful – the notion that on the night, anything could happen. Indeed, Hoy did not anticipate the Olympic record being broken trial upon trial by his competitors. Hoy explained, "Even when you feel as though everything is 100% it can still go wrong on the night so you never know for sure that you're going to do the performance you expect."[7]

Effort

It goes without saying that to perform at the elite level in this event, the requirement for effort is always high. But in an Olympic final such as Hoy found himself in, this is magnified by the sheer gravity of the occasion. In fact, Hoy recognised that, "It's such a hard thing to do… I'll never experience pressure like that again."[8] The pressure of the situation meant that not only was the event physically effortful in an extreme sense, but it was also effortful psychologically. Hoy explained, "It was the biggest challenge of my life so far; not only physically but mentally too, being able to focus in that situation wasn't easy"[9]

Remember, Hoy's task was not just to go round the track as quickly as he could. He had to do this under the immense pressure of his competitors breaking records before him, and under the pressure of an Olympic final. The mental effort required for a high pressure performance should never be underestimated.

Danger to Esteem

3.9 billion people had access to the coverage of the Athens 2004 Olympic Games and from a broadcasting perspective it was the most covered games in history up to that point.[10] So Hoy was performing in front of the world's glare. Hoy was world champion and favourite for the event, so if he lost it would be very damaging to his self-esteem. The maxim 'the bigger you are the harder you fall' is very true in sport and with so many spectators, and with the media coverage so expansive, failure for Hoy would have been very damaging indeed. He would potentially think less of himself, and others would think less of him. "The Olympics are the be all and end all," pronounced Hoy.[11]

Now, the Resources

Okay – we have had a look at the potential demands that Hoy may have been processing at the event. Now let's look at how he tipped the balance by assessing his resources (self-confidence, control, approach goals).

Self-Confidence

As previously mentioned, Hoy was the reigning world champ in this event, and as you will see in chapter 5, past performance success is a huge booster of self-confidence. If you watch the video footage of Hoy prior to the race, it is a picture of assertiveness and focus. He did not look worried or anxious – he looked ready. Have a look at the video here to assess his behaviour for yourself: https://www.youtube.com/watch?v=JzceCYkv4xQ

But the fact that he was world champion is not enough, by itself, to instil the self-belief needed for this event. It also requires in-performance confidence management. Hoy describes how, "Usually at 500m you start to feel the sting. I just had to remind myself that this is a good pain, this is a good pain. You're going well here."[12] With such statements, Hoy is using self-talk to boost his self-belief: he is having a good trial, whilst managing the pain he is experiencing. The ability for Hoy to 'verbally persuade' himself at this time was crucial for the execution of the trial, especially after the 500m mark.

Control

As you will read in chapter 6, control is all about recognizing what can, and cannot, be controlled in the performance situation, and taking advantage of those things that you can control. For example, after Tournant got an Olympic record, Hoy recalled thinking: "There's nothing I can do about that. I just have to do my own ride here."[13] In other words, Hoy knew he could not control Tournant's performance, only his own. And how did he control his own performance? He prepared as best he could and peaked at the right time, in the right place. Hoy explains, "It's just all about preparation. Making sure your body and your bike are ready for the challenge really gives you confidence."[14] From his preparation he drew confidence. By taking control of his preparation he knew that he was ready to fulfil his potential.

Achievement Goals

To be confident and focussed on what you can control is vital for performance in any sport. But the third resource - achievement goals - can help to focus that positive mindset towards victory. Hoy had been working with Dr. Steve Peters, the (then) Great Britain cycling sport psychiatrist, on his mental approach to performance. Hoy talks about working with Dr. Peters to come up with, "A strategy of dealing with the pressure. It basically involved displacing the negative thoughts with visualisation. Not a complicated technique, but very effective if done properly. I just kept running through the race in my head over and over so that I wouldn't let the distractions around me put me off."[15] Hoy was running the perfect race over and over in his head. What a positive, success-focused, strategy... *the perfect race*.

To compliment this visualisation (discussed more in chapter 5), and instead of thinking about failure or dwelling on what he might lose if he performed poorly, Hoy focussed on a very simple performance-relevant cue – his grip: "All I was thinking about was 'get a good grip'"[16] he said.

Also, remember that Hoy was the last man to race. So he knew how everyone else had performed – this would make focusing on his own race more difficult. Hoy recalled that:

"There's a lot of pressure going off as the last man...It's not really an enviable position to be in, but at the end of the day it was about focusing on my own ride and not worrying about what else has happened before me."[17]

He stayed completely focused on his own race; on producing his performance when it counted. Of course he was nervous. The demands were very high. In fact, Hoy stated that "I was more nervous than I've ever been in my whole life... To see such fast times made it very, very difficult to focus on my own ride, but it was something I had to do."[18]

Hoy was able to tip the balance by drawing on his resources. As the commentator, Hugh Porter, said at the time: "He delivered – and he delivered right on cue."[19]

Explaining The MAPP cont...

Hopefully, the important roles that demands and resources play are now clear, so let's move on to the rest of The MAPP. It may be worth looking back at The MAPP to jog your memory before we move on.

Based on the first four steps, the body responds accordingly and automatically, and we move on to the *Mind and Body Reactions* step. If our resources meet our demands (the scales tip in our favour) we experience the helpful emotions and physiological reactions that define a challenge state. If you remember from chapter 1, this includes a more efficient cardiovascular response marked by an increase in the amount of blood pumped from the heart per minute, and a decrease in vascular constriction, from normal resting levels. This is a helpful reaction for sport performance.

If our resources do not meet our demands, we experience the unhelpful emotions and physiological reactions that define a threat state. Again from chapter 1, these include a less efficient cardiovascular response marked by an unchanged or reduced amount of blood pumped from the heart per minute, and an increase in vascular constriction, from normal resting levels. This is an unhelpful reaction for performance and perhaps more crucially can prove harmful to our long-term health.[20] That is, if you react in a threat state to pressure over and over again, it can lead to all sorts of health issues. Health issues are beyond the scope of this particular book but an important consideration for those of you who may experience chronic stress in your sport. They magnify the importance of learning to approach pressure in the right way.

So, if our resources meet demands, a challenge state occurs, but if our resources do not meet the demands, a threat state occurs. This book chiefly focuses on teaching you how to perform well in tough situations, and how to increase your resources so that you can face any demands in your sport; getting into a challenge state is a huge part of this. The illustration below shows how the three resources come together to produce a challenge state. As you have probably realized, it is better to have high levels of each resource; it makes getting into a challenge state more likely.

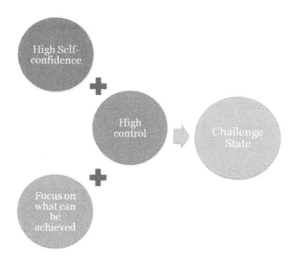

Three resources coming together to produce a challenge state

This book is about how to perform in tough situations by getting into a challenge state when it counts.

The MAPP ends with *Consequences* resulting from the accumulation of the previous steps. Predictably, in a threat state these consequences will not help to produce peak performance and in fact could potentially ruin performance.

In The MAPP, the consequences of a threat state include paralysis by analysis, ironic mental processes, and an inability to regulate attention (more on these later). Therefore, any performance requiring decision making, mental processing, physical functioning, or emotional management (think of Hoy's Athens 2004 performance) will suffer and most likely end in failure. By contrast, in a challenge state decision making, mental processing, physical functioning, and memory recall will not suffer and may be the deciding factors in your eventual success.

Based on the information covered thus far, it is possible to construct more detailed MAPPs to include some of the nuances we have picked up along the way, and to illustrate what both the challenge and threat MAPPs look like.

Paralysis by Analysis: Over-thinking skill execution, causing disrupted attention and poor skill execution.

Ironic Mental Processes: Wanting so badly not to mess-up that you tell yourself not to mess-up. Ironically, this makes failure more likely!

Challenge MAP(eak)P

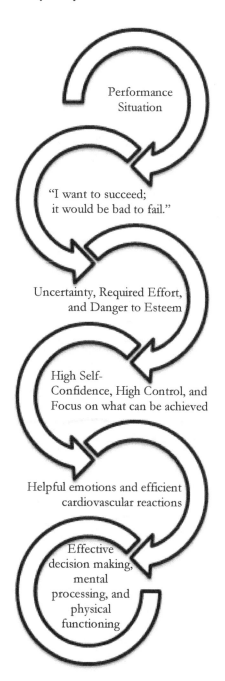

Performance Situation

"I want to succeed; it would be bad to fail."

Uncertainty, Required Effort, and Danger to Esteem

High Self-Confidence, High Control, and Focus on what can be achieved

Helpful emotions and efficient cardiovascular reactions

Effective decision making, mental processing, and physical functioning

Threat MAP(oor)P

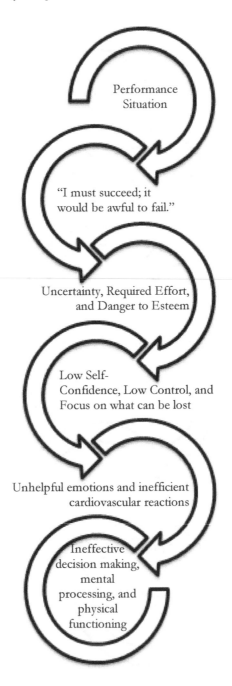

Performance Situation

"I must succeed; it would be awful to fail."

Uncertainty, Required Effort, and Danger to Esteem

Low Self-Confidence, Low Control, and Focus on what can be lost

Unhelpful emotions and inefficient cardiovascular reactions

Ineffective decision making, mental processing, and physical functioning

The first four steps of The MAPP are vitally important for getting yourself into a challenge state. By comparing the Challenge MAPP with the Threat MAPP, we can see that (apart from the first and third steps) there are key differences at each step, and it is these differences that we are interested in. More specifically, this book will help you to get on the Challenge MAPP at step 2, and keep you on the Challenge MAPP through steps 3 to 6, so that - at step 6 - you will be able to achieve peak performance.

Learning to be Challenged

As we stated in the Preface, it is advisable that you first complete all the chapters in this book, and then refer to The Challenge MAPP separately - to continue your development of the skills and techniques that lead to a challenge state and peak performance.

One possible way to get the best use out of this book is to self-assess your approach to important performance situations as they arise. This allows you to identify which areas you need to work on more than others. Remember the importance of "Knowing Thyself". To aid your self-assessment, Appendix 1 offers a short set of questions and accompanying scoring instructions. When you have answered the questions (honestly!), do the simple calculations, and you will arrive at your Challenge and Threat Score.

I think self-awareness is probably the most important thing towards being a champion.[21]

Billie Jean King, Tennis Player

Brief Summary

Let's take stock of where we are before we move on to the remaining chapters. When approaching important performance situations, such as penalty shoot-outs, Olympic trials, the final round of a golf tournament, a regional triathlon (just some examples) we can react in one of two ways: a challenge state or a threat state. A challenge state is a helpful approach and occurs when our resources (self-confidence, control, and achievement goals) meet the demands of the situation. Challenge and threat states each have their own associated bodily reactions. The challenge state's bodily reaction is more efficient for energy delivery around the body and is therefore helpful for sport performance and health. The MAPP for Success provides a guide to what causes challenge and threat states, so that you can understand what you can do to get yourself into a challenge state.

Most Important Point

You *can* control the way you react to important performance situations by learning and developing your mental skills. By increasing your resources to meet demands you can make sure you approach important performance situations in a challenge state. By doing this, you can produce peak performance more consistently, and more effectively.

---

[1] Everything negative-pressure, challenges- is all an opportunity for me to rise. (n.d.). *In brainyquote.com*. Retrieved August 16, 2014 from http://www.brainyquote.com/quotes/quotes/k/kobebryant167163.html

[2] Maya Angelou Quotes. (n.d.). *In Goodreads.com*. Retrieved May 21, 2014, from http://www.goodreads.com/quotes/13334-surviving-is-important-thriving-is-elegant

[3] The only pressure I feel is the pressure I put on myself to win. (n.d.). *In brainyquote.com*. Retrieved May 21, 2014, from http://www.brainyquote.com/quotes/quotes/a/andymurray482407.html

[4] Paula Radcliffe Quotes. (n.d.). *In searchquotes.com*. Retrieved May 21, 2014, from
http://www.searchquotes.com/quotation/For_an_athlete,_the_biggest_pr essure_comes_from_within._You_know_what_you_want_to_do_and_wha t_you're/399738/

[5] Jones, M. V., Meijen, C., McCarthy, P. J., & Sheffield, D. (2009). A theory of challenge and threat states in athletes. *International Review of Sport and Exercise Psychology, 2*, 161-180.

[6] Carrick, C. (2008). Chris Hoy: Gold medal won at Athens Olympic Games was toughest. *The Telegraph*. Retrieved May 21, 2014, from
http://www.telegraph.co.uk/sport/othersports/cycling/3185474/Chris-Hoy-Gold-medal-won-at-Athens-Olympic-Games-was-toughest-Cycling.html

[7] Sir Chris Hoy, cyclist (n. d.). *In bbc.co.uk*. Retrieved May 21, 2014, from
http://www.bbc.co.uk/wales/raiseyourgame/sites/inspiration/heroes/pag es/chris_hoy.shtml

[8] Carrick, C. (2008). Chris Hoy: Gold medal won at Athens Olympic Games was toughest. *The Telegraph*. Retrieved May 21, 2014, from
http://www.telegraph.co.uk/sport/othersports/cycling/3185474/Chris-Hoy-Gold-medal-won-at-Athens-Olympic-Games-was-toughest-Cycling.html

[9] Sir Chris Hoy, cyclist (n. d.). *In bbc.co.uk*. Retrieved May 21, 2014, from
http://www.bbc.co.uk/wales/raiseyourgame/sites/inspiration/heroes/pag es/chris_hoy.shtml

[10] International Olympic Committee. (2004). Athens 2004 Olympic Games Global Television Report. *Sports Marketing Surveys*. Retrieved May 21, 2014, from
http://www.olympic.org/documents/reports/en/en_report_1086.pdf

[11] craydee1975. (2011). *Chris Hoy's 1KM Time Trial Gold Medal at the 2004 Athens Olympics*. Retrieved May 21, 2014, from
https://www.youtube.com/watch?v=JzceCYkv4xQ

[12] craydee1975. (2011). *Chris Hoy's 1KM Time Trial Gold Medal at the 2004 Athens Olympics*. Retrieved May 21, 2014, from
https://www.youtube.com/watch?v=JzceCYkv4xQ

[13] craydee1975. (2011). *Chris Hoy's 1KM Time Trial Gold Medal at the 2004 Athens Olympics*. Retrieved May 21, 2014, from https://www.youtube.com/watch?v=JzceCYkv4xQ

[14] Sir Chris Hoy, cyclist (n. d.). *In bbc.co.uk*. Retrieved May 21, 2014, from http://www.bbc.co.uk/wales/raiseyourgame/sites/inspiration/heroes/pages/chris_hoy.shtml

[15] Sir Chris Hoy, cyclist (n. d.). *In bbc.co.uk*. Retrieved May 21, 2014, from http://www.bbc.co.uk/wales/raiseyourgame/sites/inspiration/heroes/pages/chris_hoy.shtml

[16] craydee1975. (2011). *Chris Hoy's 1KM Time Trial Gold Medal at the 2004 Athens Olympics*. Retrieved May 21, 2014, from https://www.youtube.com/watch?v=JzceCYkv4xQ

[17] Gordos, P. (2004). Hoy stands tall under pressure. *In bbc.co.uk*. Retrieved May 21, 2014, from http://news.bbc.co.uk/sport1/hi/olympics_2004/cycling/3584866.stm

[18] Gordos, P. (2004). Hoy stands tall under pressure. *In bbc.co.uk*. Retrieved May 21, 2014, from http://news.bbc.co.uk/sport1/hi/olympics_2004/cycling/3584866.stm

[19] craydee1975. (2011). *Chris Hoy's 1KM Time Trial Gold Medal at the 2004 Athens Olympics*. Retrieved May 21, 2014, from https://www.youtube.com/watch?v=JzceCYkv4xQ

[20] O'Donovan, A., Tomiyama, A. J., Lin, J., Puterman, E., Adler, N. E., Kemeny, M., Wolkowitz, O. M., Blackburn, E. H., & Epel, E. S. (2012). Stress appraisals and cellular aging: A key role for anticipatory threat in the relationship between psychological stress and telomere length. *Brain, Behavior, and Immunity*, *26*, (4), 573-579.

[21] Self-awareness quotes. (n.d.). *In brainyquote.com*. Retrieved May 21, 2014, from http://www.brainyquote.com/quotes/quotes/b/billiejean132271.html

Chapter 3: Think Smart

I'm very, very disappointed [but] it's not a tragedy, it's only a tennis match.

Rafa Nadal, Tennis Player, having lost to Lukas Rosol at Wimbledon 2012

Nadal is only human.

Lukas Rosol, Tennis Player, following his victory

In the second round of the 2012 Wimbledon tennis championships, former champion and World Number Two (at the time) Rafa Nadal was matched against World Number 100 - Lukas Rosol. By all accounts this was a match that Nadal should have won, comfortably. Indeed, Rosol was making his main draw debut at Wimbledon, whilst Nadal had won in 2008 and 2010.

In the first set, Nadal worked hard against Rosol to win a tie-break 11-9 with an emphatic forehand winner. But Rosol seemed un-phased and continued to play with confidence and conviction, breaking Nadal in the first game of the second set and taking the set 6-4.

Rosol continued his assault on Nadal in the third set, took an early break, and made it two sets to one. Rosol's game then started to show signs of inconsistency, and Nadal took advantage to win the fourth set. Dramatically, the match was then halted due to poor light, so that the roof could be closed. The players returned 43 minutes later at which point Rosol broke Nadal immediately and managed to hold on to secure a shock victory on Centre Court.[1]

Fast forward to Wimbledon 2013.

Nadal was drawn in round one against Steve Darcis, ranked 135 in the world. Again, surely an easy win for Nadal who, up to this point, had never lost in the first round of a Grand Slam. In the first set, Darcis managed to get break points on Nadal's first three service games, and converted one to lead 6-5. Nadal broke back immediately and a tie-break was set up. Darcis took it 7-4. He then repeated this unlikely event in the second set to make it 2-0. Nadal was clearly in trouble and errors started to appear in his backhand. He then began to limp and it became obvious that he was injured. Darcis started to play with real confidence at this point and finished Nadal off unequivocally. In fact Darcis won 86 percent of his first-serve points in the deciding set. Nadal's response after losing this match?[2]

"I tried my best and congratulate the opponent. It is not a tragedy, it is sport."[3]

Even more recently (April 2014), Nadal's 41-match winning streak came to an abrupt end when he lost in three sets to Nicolas Almargo in the quarter finals of the Barcelona Open. Nadal is considered the greatest clay court player of all time, and had not lost in Barcelona since he was 15 years old. Can you guess his reaction?

"Tennis is just a game."[4]

Regardless of the circumstances (e.g., injury in the case of Wimbledon 2013) that led to Nadal's defeat in all three instances, Nadal's reactions to failure can teach us a lot about how to deal with setbacks and, also, how to approach important situations.

As humans, we fail. We are fallible, but this does not mean we are *failures*. Chapter 3 urges you to *Think Smart*. By Think Smart we do not mean - be more intelligent. We are not alluding to some sort of IQ boosting strategy. Think Smart is about being logical and pragmatic in your philosophies and beliefs. By Thinking Smart you will be able to approach your sporting events in the right frame of mind for success, and will prove able to deal with setbacks constructively and with poise when it matters most. Just like Rafa!

Woman Troubles

We want to really kick off this chapter by telling a story that, although it has nothing to do with sport, has everything to do with Think Smart!

Meet Al. Al lives in New York City and is painfully shy of women. In fact, Al is quite angry about his inability to talk to women he finds attractive for fear of rejection. He has a social phobia that causes him to avoid situations where he would have to talk to women.

Then, he decides enough is enough and he is going to conquer his fear. One sunny day he hangs around near a bench in the New York Botanical Garden in the Bronx. He speaks to every single woman who sits down alone within one minute of them appearing there. Normally, he would get scared and not approach women for conversation. However, having made his commitment to overcome his fears, he approaches 130 women over the course of one month.

Al risked failure and rejection, and did what was most uncomfortable for him. He gave himself no time to procrastinate about approaching the women, and no time to worry about the consequences (e.g., rejection and humiliation).

Thirty women walked away instantly, not giving him a chance to even get started. He talked with another 100 women for the first time in his life, no matter how anxious he felt. Out of all the women he talked to, he was able to make one date... who didn't show up. But nobody vomited, nobody died, nobody ran away. Nobody called the cops.[5]

With this, Al realized that his fear of talking to women was based on illogical beliefs about rejection and humiliation. His old thinking was that rejection would be awful and unbearable. But he got over his shyness and social phobia by thinking differently, feeling differently and, in particular, acting differently. He faced his fears and proved scientifically that there is nothing terrible about rejection.

Al, or Dr. Albert Ellis, went on to conceive Rational Emotive Behaviour Therapy (REBT), the first cognitive behavioural therapy.[6]

Think Smart is based on the ideas of Dr. Albert Ellis and on the success of REBT principles in helping millions of people achieve

41

their goals. The main principle is this: *It is not the situations you face that cause unhelpful emotions, it is the way you think about those situations.*[7]

It just so happens that the way we think about sport performances is very often illogical: causing unhelpful emotions and destructive behaviours that prohibit our goal achievement. As sport psychology consultants, we see this in athletes all the time. The coach drops the athlete from the team and "it's *awful*", a big match approaches and they "absolutely *must* play well". In our work we have found a way to help athletes approach, and deal with, performance in a more balanced way. A Smarter way.

It is not the situation that causes unhelpful emotions, it is the way you think about those situations.

Thought Experiment

Okay, let's continue this chapter with a thought experiment.[8]

Experiment 1: We want you to imagine that you have $10 in your pocket. We also want you to hold the belief that you would *like* to have a minimum of $11 in your pocket at all times. Really try to ingrain this belief, this want for $11 at all times. Repeat it like a mantra if it helps (e.g., "I have $10 but would really *like* to have at least $11 in my pocket at all times"). You would like to have $11, but *it's not the end of the world* that you only have $10.

Make a mental note of how you feel in this instance.

Experiment 2: Now, just like before, imagine you have $10, but this time hold the belief that you absolutely *must*, at all times, have a minimum of $11 in your pocket. Again, really try to hold this belief and perhaps use the mantra: "I have $10, but I *must* always have at least $11". You must have $11, and *it is terrible* that you only have $10.

Once again, make a mental note of how you feel in this instance.

The situation you imagined did not change between experiment 1 and experiment 2. The only thing that changed was the philosophy or belief you held. But most probably, you reported different feelings in experiment 1 when compared to experiment 2. Maybe you were worried at not having $11 in experiment 1, but panicked in experiment 2? The point here is not really about money. It's about how your philosophies and beliefs (I *would like* $11 vs. I *must have* $11) influence how you feel, even when the situation is identical.

The thought experiments you just completed show how rigid and illogical demands (I *must…*) can lead to unhelpful approaches and reactions even in everyday situations. When these demands are magnified by important events in your sport and pressure performance situations, the unhelpful approaches and reactions are also magnified. So, in a relatively tame situation such as not having enough money for a cab you may experience anxiety due to your demands. But in more meaningful and potentially life-changing events such as a cup final or championship match, you may experience severe and highly debilitating anxiety due to those rigid demands.

The key point we want you to take from chapter 3 is that it is not the situation that causes the anxiety, or the anger, or the depressed feelings, it is the philosophy or beliefs you have *about* the situation. This is really important because it means that you are not a slave to your emotional reactions in any situation. You have control over your emotions because you can control your philosophies and beliefs. To illustrate, it's as simple as ABC.

---

*Our philosophy or beliefs about a situation
influence our emotions.*

Chapter 3

ABC

Many athletes think and talk like this: "Competitions make me feel anxious" or "The coach's behaviour towards me made me angry". If you think of the situation (competition/coach's behaviour) as "A" and the response (anxiety/anger) as "C", the following illustrates such thinking:

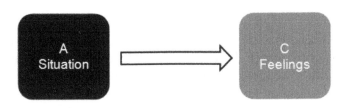

This A-C way of thinking is problematic for two main reasons.

1. *It's not true.* The only time a situation directly generates feelings is when something genuinely disastrous occurs (e.g., natural disaster), or when something occurs very suddenly (the fear experienced when a spider comes out from under your sofa [if you are afraid of spiders, and even then, this fear is based on your deep-down beliefs about spiders]) and there simply isn't time to consciously process the event.

2. It suggests that something, or somebody, has *control* over you and your responses. No one can 'make you' feel angry, not even your coach. There is a staggering amount of mental processing to be done before you become angry, and it rarely has anything to do with the situation itself; it has more to do with your beliefs *about* that situation. This is why *we* may get angry at certain occurrences, while a teammate may remain completely calm. If the anger directly stemmed from the situation, we would all be angry at precisely the same things, which isn't the case.

This A-C way of thinking leaves out a really important part of how we actually react to pressure and adversity – your beliefs.

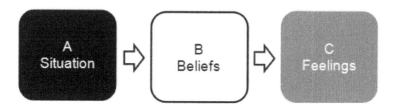

It is your philosophy, or beliefs about the situation, that dictate your reactions to it. Dr. Albert Ellis referred to a Greek philosopher Epictetus who put forth the famous maxim of: "People are disturbed not by things, but by the view which they take of them."

Put simply, it is not the situation (A) alone that causes your emotional reactions (C); it is what you tell yourself (B) about that situation that is mostly to blame.

This ABC way of thinking is helpful in one major way. It means that you can control your emotional reactions to situations when you want to be at the top of your game by altering the way you think about the situation you are approaching. So all you need to do is identify problem philosophies and beliefs, and swap them for helpful philosophies and beliefs.[9]

But what are these 'problem' philosophies and beliefs? What do they look like and what could they lead to? How do you replace philosophies and beliefs? Let's answer these questions next.

Problem Philosophies and Beliefs

When Thinking Smart, your beliefs are rational, logical, and pragmatic. So when you are not Thinking Smart, you are thinking destructively; your beliefs are irrational, illogical, and unpragmatic.

Destructive Thinking involves very specific beliefs,
known to cause unhealthy emotions that
hinder your chances of thriving when it matters
most – causing self-destructive behaviours.

Here is a comparison of Destructive Thinking versus Smart Thinking:

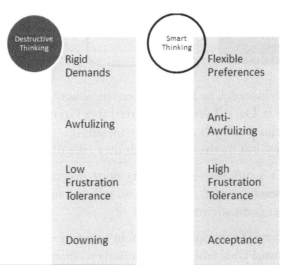

Destructive Thinking

As mentioned above, Destructive Thinking involves irrational, illogical, and unpragmatic beliefs. But let's be more specific.

1. **Rigid Demands**: "I must succeed in big matches" | "I must be treated fairly"

2. **Awfulizing**: "Failure is awful/terrible" | "Being treated disrespectfully is awful/terrible"

3. **Low Frustration Tolerance**: "I can't stand being treated with disrespect" | "I cannot tolerate unfairness"

4. **Downing**: "Failing makes me a failure" | "If I fail it goes to show what an idiot I am"

You have probably spotted some familiar phrases above. Perhaps you use phrases similar to these when you compete or train in your sport? But maybe you hadn't realized the potential danger of holding such beliefs when approaching competitions or dealing with setbacks.

It is important to make clear, at this point, that unhealthy emotions occur only when these phrases reflect deeply held beliefs. That is, you might say "I must succeed" but not really mean it. Destructive Thinking is only an issue when the beliefs are genuinely held. Research has shown that these irrational, illogical, and unpragmatic thoughts can lead to severe emotional issues such as phobias, chronic depression, and even suicidal thoughts.[10, 11]

A fascinating, illuminating, and very sad documentary aired on the BBC in the U.K. in 2013. It was an investigation into depression and suicide in English soccer. The Chairman of the Professional Footballers' Association - Clarke Carlisle - led the investigation, having struggled with depression across his life, even attempting to take his own life after a serious injury. His thoughts on his situation hinted at some harmful beliefs. For example: "My self-confidence and self-esteem in particular are inextricably linked with football. Losing a game makes me feel low."[12] This is a good example of A-C thinking, where the emotion and behaviour stem directly from the event.

In the documentary Ronald Reng talked about his close friend German goalkeeper Robert Enke, his struggle with depression, and his suicide in 2009 at the age of 32. "In his case it was the particular pressure he put himself under as a goalkeeper to always be perfect, to never make mistakes. He put himself so much under pressure 'I need to be Barcelona's number one goal keeper.'" Again, rigid and demanding beliefs predominated. We are not suggesting that rigid and demanding beliefs always lead to depression. But it is important to highlight that there is a serious side to illogical thinking.

Let's look back at The MAPP from chapter 2. In The MAPP, your philosophy feeds directly into your perceptions of situational demands. More specifically, holding irrational, illogical, and unpragmatic philosophies and beliefs causes distorted perceptions of demands. By having a belief such as: "I must succeed and it would be terrible if I failed", the perceived danger present in the situation is magnified. Not danger in a physical sense, but danger to esteem, danger of embarrassment, a danger of letting yourself and others down.

By demanding success so rigidly, and by considering the consequences of failure to be terrible, you have created, in your mind, a situation in which failure goes against a fundamental rule or law. It is no wonder that this Destructive Thinking leads to severe emotions. In addition, and importantly, by demanding success, or fair treatment, or respect, you set yourself up for disappointment because no demand can be fulfilled for sure and indefinitely. This is why we asked you about your beliefs in The MAPP questionnaire in chapter 2 (see the appendix).

The good news is that there are some highly effective strategies for dealing with Destructive Thinking. Remember, because your emotional reactions are a result of your philosophies and beliefs (B), all you need to do is to change B to change your reactions. Changing B (i.e., developing a new philosophy or belief about a situation) involves a 6-step Smart Thinking process where you challenge your beliefs and eradicate Destructive Thinking.

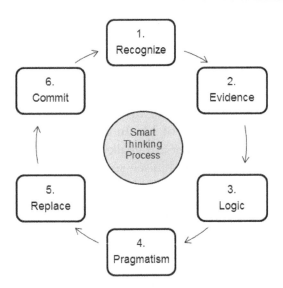

1. Recognize

When you feel anxious or angry or depressed - ask yourself this question: "What am I telling myself about the situation (A) that is causing my unhelpful reaction (C)?"

This question will help you to recognize the demands ("I must!") you hold, and also whether you are awfulizing ("It would be awful if..."), showing signs of low frustration tolerance ("I can't stand it when..."), and/or self-downing ("I am a failure"). You can try this now.

Think back to a time in your sport when you were particularly anxious, angry, or depressed. It could be in training, or in competition. Think about the situation that prompted these emotions, and ask: "What was I telling myself about A that caused C". You are using A and C to find B. From our work with elite athletes we find this question to be one of the most effective mechanisms for beginning the process of Smart Thinking. Many athletes report this to be a mantra that they take with them and use across various situations (including training, competition, and even at home).

For example, a tennis athlete who is unjustly penalized (A) by an umpire may become angry and violent (C) due to telling herself (B) that she "must be treated fairly" and she "can't stand it" when she is not.

Once you have found B (e.g., "I must... and it would be terrible if..."), then the next step is to commit to changing it.

2. Evidence

Once you have recognized the specific problem - B - you can now move on to challenging this philosophy, starting with the search for proof.

In step 2 you are asking "where is the evidence that I must...?" and "where is the evidence that it would be terrible if...?"

A useful way to search for evidence is to think of a time when you have failed, or have been treated unfairly or with disrespect. Most successful athletes have failed at some point in their lives. Michael Jordan is a great example of a legendary athlete who didn't always succeed. Jordan famously said, "I've missed more than 9000 shots in my career. I've lost almost 300 games. 26 times, I've been trusted to take the game winning shot and missed. I've failed over and over and over again in my life. And that is why I succeed."[13] Jordan also said that, "I can accept failure, everyone fails at something."[14] It is not failure in itself that threatens to derail your rise to the top; it is really how you respond to failure that is the key factor here. Remember, David Beckham was once labelled 'one stupid little boy' by some of the U.K.'s press following his sending off against Argentina at the World Cup in 1998. But now Beckham is remembered for bouncing back from that adversity to become a more complete athlete. Look at the performance history of your favourite athletes and you will find adversity and failure, but importantly, the ability to come back stronger.

Humans are fallible and therefore every athlete fails.

The ability to think of just one occurrence of failure or mistreatment fundamentally disproves your necessity to succeed, be treated fairly, or with respect. After all, by saying that you must succeed, for example, and if you really believe it, you are actually saying that you are bound (guaranteed) by an imperative (vital) requirement (necessity) to succeed.

How can success be a guaranteed vital requirement if you can think of times when you have failed? You are still here (reading this book). You did not perish in consequence to your past failures. There is no evidence to support demands for success, fairness, or respect.

If we take the athlete from step 1, for example, it is unlikely that this was the first time she had been treated unfairly, and the fact that she is still alive despite previous mistreatment shows that she can in fact 'stand it' and that her demand to be treated fairly is inconsistent with past experiences; it is not based on evidence.

3. Logic

Searching for logic is about searching for sense. The rigidity of Destructive Thinking rarely reflects reality, save a few notable exceptions. Spend a moment thinking about all the things you must have, or must do, in this world. Really think about this, and be critical. All the things you *must* have, or *must* do.

Typically, people suggest the following things: food, air, water, shelter, and sleep. Even this list of necessities is open to debate, with many people living without shelter (with difficulty admittedly). The point here is that success, being treated fairly and with respect does not belong in this list of crucial needs. Compared to the list, success, fairness, and respect are more of a luxury than a need. So *logically*, the word 'must' does not apply to success, fairness, and respect, and we are erroneous in our ways when applying rigid demands to such luxurious things.

For the unfairly treated tennis athlete, for example, her belief does not reflect reality because if she had to be treated fairly, unfair treatment would be the end of her. Fair treatment from an umpire, or anyone else, does not belong with life's necessities.

At this stage in the process you have learned how to challenge Destructive Thinking both evidentially and logically. But just in case you need more convincing to change Destructive Thinking, next we will think pragmatically.

4. Pragmatism

This is all about asking the question: "Where is this belief getting me?" In other words, if you are getting anxious on the approach to competitions, angry when you feel mistreated by an official, or depressed when dropped from the team, then why not change Destructive Thinking and change these reactions?

For the tennis athlete, clearly an angry and violent response is not helpful. Reactions such as this often lead to disciplinary action against athletes, and can also ruin the athlete's focus for the rest of the match, hindering their performance. So the rigid demand for fairness and the belief that unfair treatment is intolerable is unpragmatic.

51

Fundamentally, if you are experiencing unhelpful emotional reactions, then it is B that is causing this, not the situation (A). So B is evidently not helping you.

It is important at this point to understand that the emotions we refer to here - anxiety, anger, depression - are unhelpful and unhealthy. This is because they lead to unconstructive actions that do not aid you in your goals and aspirations in your sport. Of course, when approaching competitions you will feel nervous, and when slighted or treated with disrespect you will feel frustrated or sad. But Smart Thinking is about reacting in a constructive way, and not necessarily with positive emotions (happiness or excitement). So nervousness, frustration, and sadness can be used constructively, whereas anxiety, anger, and depression cannot. To make this idea simpler, we have organized beliefs and reactions in the below table, based on Dr. Albert Ellis' ground-breaking ideas.

Where are my beliefs getting me?

Example Situation (A)	Type of belief (B)	Healthy or unhealthy	Emotion (C)	Behaviour (C)
Important championship competition	Destructive	Unhealthy	Anxiety	Withdraw mentally and physically
	Smart	Healthy	Concern	Face up to situation and take constructive action
Being unfairly and unjustly reprimanded or blamed. Your goal obstructed or prohibited	Destructive	Unhealthy	Unhealthy anger	Aggressively attack other people, physically and or verbally
	Smart	Healthy	Healthy anger	Assert self and request behavioural change from other people
Being let down or failing in an important situation	Destructive	Unhealthy	Depression	Withdraw and try to terminate feelings in self-destructive ways
	Smart	Healthy	Sadness	Express and talk about feelings to teammates, friends and relatives

So pragmatism is about realizing that Destructive Thinking leads to unhelpful emotions and behaviours. Therefore, Destructive Thinking is unpragmatic. Destructive Thinking will not help you reach your goals. Maybe you can spot some of your behaviours (C) in the table – if so, track back and explore your Bs.

Here is some wisdom from Brad Gilbert, the tennis coach who coached Andy Roddick, that helps to illustrate our point:

"The one thing you can control is working hard, competing hard and having a good time. If you tell yourself, 'I gotta win here, I gotta win there', you set yourself up for crash and burn. It's all about trying to get better. What is OK is when you lose to the other guy, what is not OK is when you lose to yourself."[15]

So, why retain self-defeating beliefs if they are unhelpful? Why not *replace* them?

5. Replace

It is important to first successfully challenge your Destructive Thinking before replacing your philosophies and beliefs with Smart Thinking. The reason to reject Destructive Thinking is because it is irrational, illogical, and unpragmatic; so it stands to reason that Smart Thinking is about being rational, logical, and pragmatic. Let's be more specific.

Smart Thinking

1. **Flexible Thinking**: "I want to succeed in important competitions" | "I want to be treated fairly, but don't have to be"

2. **Anti-Awfulizing**: "Failure is bad, but not awful/terrible" | "Being treated disrespectfully is bad but not awful"

3. **High Frustration Tolerance**: "I don't like being treated with disrespect, but that doesn't mean it shouldn't happen" | "Just because I don't like unfairness doesn't mean I should be treated fairly"

4. **Acceptance**: "Failing does not make me a failure" | "If I fail, it does not mean I am an idiot"

So the tennis athlete's belief "I must be treated fairly, and I can't stand it when I am not" becomes "I want to be treated fairly, but that doesn't mean I have to be, and I *can* tolerate unfair treatment."

As you will have noticed, Smart Thinking is the opposite of Destructive Thinking. But the most important part of changing Destructive Thinking to Smart Thinking is that you *challenge* Smart Thinking just like you challenged Destructive Thinking. It is crucial that you test your Smart Thinking for evidence, logic, and pragmatics. It's only fair that your new philosophies are scrutinized too!

Destructive vs. Smart

To aid you in your quest to eradicate Destructive Thinking, it may be helpful to directly compare Destructive Thinking and the Smart alternative. Let's take the belief "I must always succeed and it is awful when I fail" and do a comparison.

Destructive	Smart
"I must always succeed and it is awful when I fail"	"I want to always succeed, but failure isn't awful"
Evidence: Nowhere is it written that I must succeed, and I have failed before so my demand for success is unfounded. For failure to be awful, it would have to be worse than 100% bad. This isn't possible.	Evidence: Of course I want to always succeed, and my strong preferences, instead of rigid demands, do not mean that I want it any less. Failure is not awful; it is not even the worst thing I can think of, so it can't be awful.

Logic:	Logic:
It is nonsensical that just because I demand success I will get it. Success is not a necessity like food, water, or air, so how can I make such demands for it? Saying that failure is awful suggests that there is nothing worse that could possibly happen that would be worse than failure. After all, awful means 101% bad (need more convincing? Go to the "Badness Barometer").	It makes sense that I want to succeed because my preference for success is a testament to my motivation to prevail rather than my desperation for success. Failure isn't awful because nothing can be awful. Awfulness only exists in the human mind; nothing can be 101% bad (need more convincing? Go to the "Badness Barometer").
Pragmatism:	Pragmatism:
To place such rigid and inflexible demands on success is unhelpful, there is no room to budge, and treating success as a necessity is unrealistic and adds unneeded pressure to an already important situation. So there is no point in holding this Destructive Thinking.	To want to succeed is obviously helpful. Even if I want to succeed more than anything else in the world and it is a really strong preference, it is motivational but not a demand. Because I would prefer to succeed and not demand to, the pressure is manageable and the situation is not "life or death".
Conclusion:	Conclusion:
This belief is not supported by evidence, logic, **nor** pragmatism.	This belief is supported by evidence, logic, and pragmatism.

The Badness Barometer

Before we introduce this enigmatic tool, we would like you to write down 12 events that have occurred in your sport and in your life to date. Specifically, all the events should be bad, that is, they should all be negative experiences at face value. Write down a range from what you consider to be the worst thing ever to happen to you, to everyday annoyances and bad occurrences. Move on when you have done your list.

Now on to the Badness Barometer.[16]

This tool is extremely effective at destroying your Destructive Thinking. The Badness Barometer helps you to put events into perspective, helping you to realize the futility of your Destructive Thinking. Below, you will find a barometer that ranges from 0 to 100. We want you to place each of the 12 events that you listed on the Badness Barometer in relation to how bad you think the event is: 0 (not bad at all) to 100 (worst thing ever). Be very critical and place all of the events on the Badness Barometer now.

What you will probably notice is that failures and demands in your sport are not at the top of the Badness Barometer. In fact, quite often when we do this activity with professional athletes, failures and demands in their sport populate the 40-60 area of the Badness Barometer. The point is this: How can you say things like "Failure is terrible/awful" when you don't even place them at the top of your Badness Barometer? The right hand side of the Badness Barometer represents the worst possible events, but frequently we use "terrible" and "awful" to describe failures and demands in sport that are insignificant compared to some of the really bad life events we may face (which, by the way, are often not "awful" either!).

This tool is useful to help gain perspective and challenge your philosophies logically. As Boris Becker said after losing to Peter Doohan in the second round of Wimbledon in 1987: "I didn't lose a war. Nobody died. I lost a tennis match"[17], and as the former NFL player Michael Ditka said: "Failure isn't Fatal."[18]

6. Commit

Whilst recognizing and challenging your illogical philosophies and beliefs may be an eye-opening experience, our research has shown that *the more* you practice your ABCs and challenge your beliefs, the better you will be at maintaining your Smart Thinking.[19]

Smart Thinking requires commitment and frequent practice.

We have found that athletes who are exposed to Smart Thinking only once are not able to maintain their Smart Thinking. When they go through the steps more frequently, they show long-term changes in Destructive Thinking. It's really about *commitment* to changing your beliefs in order to dictate your emotional and behavioural reactions. We suggest three ways to ensure that your Smart Thinking sticks:

1. Practice the ABC often and with intent. After a tough day's training, spend ten minutes thinking about, or even jotting down, instances when you may have experienced unhelpful emotions or behaved in an unconstructive manner. Perhaps you snapped at a teammate for fouling you. Perhaps the coach said something derogatory to you after training. Find your A (event) and C (emotion/behaviour) first. It matters not about the order that you recognize your A and C. You may remember being angry recently (C) and then start to

think about the situation (A) that triggered this reaction. Then ask yourself the key question: "What was I telling myself about A that caused C". This will help you find your belief (B). Then challenge that belief using evidence, logic, and pragmatism.

2. Once you become proficient in recognizing and challenging your Destructive Thinking, you can reinforce your Smart Thinking by using Smart *self-talk*. You can do this by creating, and writing down, your Smart Thinking beliefs for use when you need them. For example, after going through the Smart Thinking process you change the Destructive belief: "I must be treated with respect" to the Smart belief "I want to be treated with respect, but that doesn't mean I have to be". You then take this Smart belief and use it as self-talk in situations where you feel you are being disrespected. In addition, after some time you will no doubt create many Smart Thinking self-talk cues. It is useful to remind yourself of these every now and again. We recommend writing them down on slips of paper or post-it notes and keeping them in a jar or your kit bag. Every now and again take a slip out and read the statement, reminding you of your Smart Thinking.

3. Seek events that typically trigger your unhelpful emotions - like Albert Ellis on the park bench facing his fears by talking to more than 100 women. By confronting your fears you will be able to prove that nothing terrible will happen as a consequence. This strengthens your Smart Thinking because you can challenge your Destructive Thinking with your own data. That is, if you are fearful of failing in front of your coach, you probably realize intellectually that it is illogical and unpragmatic (your coach does not represent a physical threat). Nothing terrible will happen – sure, it won't do you any favours, but you'll live. But by pushing yourself in training so that failure is a risk – or even a likelihood – you will have evidence that nothing terrible happens. Match this experience with your Smart Thinking (e.g., "If I fail in front of my coach it's bad, but not the end of the world!") and your fears will fade into the past. To illustrate, one cricket batsman we worked with was so fearful of failing in front of his coach, that he only ever attempted easy and safe shots. So we

encouraged him to put himself into situations that showed off his weaknesses in front of the coach. Predictably, the athlete failed more in training, but the coach's response was not to criticise the athlete or treat the athlete "terribly" – the opposite happened – the coach offered constructive advice and commended him for his fearless approach to training.

The unfairly treated tennis athlete may use visualization to imagine future occurrences of mistreatment so she can practice her ABC. Then she can develop some self-talk statements such as "Just because I want fair treatment, doesn't mean I have to get it" or "I can tolerate unfairness, I have been treated unfairly before and I am still here!". She could even set up drills with her coach where she is given poor decisions in training to learn to use the Smart Thinking process when performing. As with everything in this book, just like the physical skills you have honed through hours and hours of training in your sport, practice is imperative.

Smart Summary

You have worked hard in this chapter. Challenging your philosophies and beliefs is a worthwhile endeavour, but it is hard work. Remember, mental skills are like physical skills - they take time to learn and get better with practice.

Looking back at The MAPP we can see that step 2 is well underway. Adopting Smart Thinking is important because it feeds into your perceptions of demands. If you perceive high demands because of your rigid and distorted philosophies, you may tip the balance in the wrong direction and end up in a threat state – not good! So it's really vital for your progress to learn to Think Smart about your performance.

We want to end chapter 3 with a great example of how Smart Thinking can be used to deal with tough times. Let's return to Rory McIlroy's extraordinary meltdown on the final day of the 2011 Masters (see chapter 1). As we know, McIlroy was leading the field when he got to the 10th hole but a poor sequence of shots on the hole dropped McIlroy from first place to seventh, and he finished the round with 80.

McIlroy's response?

"There are lot of worse things that can happen in your life... Shooting a bad score in the last round of golf tournament is nothing in comparison to what other people go through."[20]

McIlroy was able to win the next major golf tournament (the US Open) in resounding fashion, shattering the tournament scoring record and winning by eight strokes.

Chapter 3, and indeed this book, encourages you to gain perspective, to take charge of your thoughts and beliefs, and to work hard to master your mental approach and responses when it matters most.

Most Important Point

It is not the cup final, failure in front of scouts, or mistreatment by an official or opponent that causes your feelings and behaviours. It is your philosophies and beliefs that lead you to feeling anxious, depressed, and angry. Change your beliefs, to change your reactions to adversity.

---

[1] Rafael Nadal falls to shock Wimbledon defeat by Lukas Rosol. (2012, June 28). *In BBC sport tennis.* Retrieved May 21, 2014, from http://www.bbc.co.uk/sport/0/tennis/18627648

[2] Rafael Nadal says Wimbledon 2013 defeat is 'not a tragedy'. (2013, June 25). *In BBC sport tennis.* Retrieved May 21, 2014, from http://www.bbc.co.uk/sport/0/tennis/23040542

[3] No excuses from gracious Nadal. (2013, June 25). *The Express.* Retrieved May 21, 2014, from http://www.express.co.uk/sport/tennis/410101/No-excuses-from-gracious-Nadal

[4] Rafael Nadal's winning streak in Barcelona is ended by Nicolas Almagro. (2014, April 25). *Edition: Open Court.* Retrieved May 21, 2014, from

http://edition.cnn.com/2014/04/25/sport/tennis/tennis-nadal-barcelona-loss/

[5] The origins of REBT. (2006, May). *REBT network*. Retrieved May 21, 2014, from http://www.rebtnetwork.org/ask/may06.html

[6] Ellis, A. (1957). Rational psychotherapy and individual psychology. *Journal of Individual Psychology, 13*, 38-44.

[7] Ellis, A., & Dryden, W. (1997). *The practice of rational-emotive behavior therapy.* New York: Springer Publishing Company.

[8] Ellis, A., & Dryden, W. (1997). *The practice of rational-emotive behavior therapy.* New York: Springer Publishing Company.

[9] Ellis, A., Gordon, J., Neenan, M., & Palmer, S. (1997). *Stress counselling: A rational emotive behavior approach.* London: Cassell.

[10] Browne, C. M., Dowd, E. T., & Freeman, A. (2010). Rational and irrational beliefs and psychopathology. In D. David, S. J. Lynn, & A. Ellis, A. (Eds.), *Rational and irrational beliefs in human functioning and disturbances: Implications for research, theory, and practice.* New York: Oxford University Press.

[11] Szentagotai, A., & Jones, J. (2010). The behavioral consequences of irrational beliefs. In D. David, S. J. Lynn, & A. Ellis (Eds.), *Rational and irrational beliefs in human functioning and disturbances.* Oxford: Oxford University Press.

[12] Keele, A. (Director). (2013, July 9). *Football's Suicide Secret* [Television broadcast]. London: BBC.

[13] Michael Jordan Quotes (n. d.). *In Goodreads.com.* Retrieved May 21, 2014, from https://www.goodreads.com/author/quotes/16823.Michael_Jordan

[14] Michael Jordan Quotes (n. d.). *In Goodreads.com.* Retrieved May 21, 2014, from https://www.goodreads.com/author/quotes/16823.Michael_Jordan

[15] Atkin, R. (2003, June 29). Roddick has the look of a believer. *The Independent.* Retrieved May 21, 2014, from http://www.independent.co.uk/sport/tennis/roddick-has-the-look-of-a-believer-110920.html

[16] Ellis, A., & Dryden, W. (1997). *The practice of rational-emotive behavior therapy.* New York: Springer Publishing Company.

[17] Zolbol. (2009, November 16). Zolbol's Tennis Special 34 - Philosophical Becker [Video file]. Retrieved May 21, 2014, from http://www.youtube.com/watch?v=kNUi4SIDEnM

[18] Adler, J. (2006, May). *Mike Ditka*. Retrieved May 21, 2014, from http://football.about.com/cs/legends/p/mikeditka.htm

[19] Turner, M. J., Slater, M. J., & Barker, J. B. (in press). The season-long effects of rational emotive behavior therapy on the irrational beliefs of professional academy soccer athletes. *International Journal of Sport Psychology*.

[20] Telegraph Staff. (2011, April 11). The Masters 2011: Rory McIlroy insists he will come back stronger after painful collapse on final round in Augusta. *The Telegraph*. Retrieved May 21, 2014, from http://www.telegraph.co.uk/sport/golf/mastersaugusta/8442210/The-Masters-2011-Rory-McIlroy-insists-he-will-come-back-stronger-after-painful-collapse-on-final-round-in-Augusta.html

Chapter 4: Tip The Balance

I am always fascinated to watch how a guy handles a pressure situation. Some players become animated, some train extra hard, some withdraw – but the true greats keep their self-belief, trust themselves and continue to work away, knowing that if the foundations have been established, good form will come.[1]

Steve Waugh, Cricketer, 2005

Above, Steve Waugh, inducted into the International Cricket Council Hall of Fame in 2010, appears to pre-empt the notion of "resources" introduced in The MAPP in chapter 2. Resources represent mental factors known to be crucial for sport performance, and are an amalgamation of scientific research and real-world insights into how athletes achieve peak performance. Here is a reminder of what the resources are:

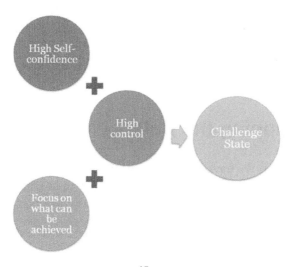

Resources

Resources are the key to getting into a challenge state and the key to performing to your potential. So tipping the balance is about enhancing your self-confidence and control, and ensuring you are always focused on what can be achieved instead of what could be lost. Increasing these three factors will tip the balance in favour of a challenge state and away from a threat state.

As resources are increased, demands are outweighed; therefore a challenge state is achieved. This is easier to achieve if you are Thinking Smart so that the demands are not magnified. As we have discussed, Smart Thinking has important implications for your physiological reactions to adversity, and ultimately affects your performance. This chapter, and subsequent ones, are all geared towards helping you learn and develop the skills you need to increase and maintain the resources for top sports performance.

Does Tipping the Balance Work?

Over the years, we have worked with many athletes on "tipping the balance", and have even put athletes through their paces in our laboratory (other sport psychology researchers around the world have done the same[2,3]) to test whether heightened resources do indeed lead to a challenge state. It is clear that athletes who evaluate an upcoming competition as a challenge perform better.

But how can resources be increased? To be clear, we know that tipping the balance is about having high self-confidence, high perceived control, and focusing on approach goals[4] but how can you, starting today, increase these important mental states?

We have developed the notion of "tipping the balance" through years of consultancy work and have also tested it in our laboratories. Increasing your resources does not involve changing how you perceive a situation. It is more about how you perceive yourself and your skills. Thriving when it matters most is not about saying: "Don't worry about it, it will be fine, that Olympic selection trial is not that important!" but is more about saying, "Okay, this is massively important, but I have what it takes to be successful here!"

We want to recount the stories of two athletes we have worked with when a threat state was causing problems for performance. Our strategy was to help the athletes to tip the balance by changing the way they thought about themselves and their skills in those pressure situations – through integrating resources into their mental preparation.

To do this, we helped them to re-appraise or re-evaluate their resources and we monitored their progress using cardiovascular measures. It is hoped that through these examples, you will be able to see how a challenge state can be promoted in practice to the benefit of performance.

Tipping the balance is about having high self-confidence, high perceived control, and focusing on approach goals.

Tim the Golfer

Visualization lets you concentrate on all the positive aspects of your game[5]

Curtis Strange, Golfer

Tim (not his real name) wanted help with his golf game. He was okay around the course on most occasions, but there was one very specific area in which he had a real problem. When putting, he was fine from medium distances, obviously long distances were tough, but when the putt was 6 feet in length, he choked. For some reason this simple putt was destroyed by his anxiety in performance situations (more of this later in the book). The issue stemmed from a number of poor putts in competitive circumstances that snowballed into really intense anxiety whenever he was required to putt at short length.

This anxiety and panic manifested in negative thoughts about the putt and physical reactions such as sweaty palms, muscle tension, and nausea.

After an initial meeting with Tim, we decided to hook him up to our cardiovascular monitor and see what happened when he imagined facing this dreaded short putt. We guided him through the imagery (visualization) of the putt using a script. His cardiovascular data showed that he was threatened when he thought about having to approach this shot. On three separate occasions we saw his Cardiac Output decrease and his Total Peripheral Resistance increase from resting levels, so we knew he was approaching this situation in a threat state for sure. *The body doesn't lie.* As we have already discussed, this was a certain sign that he was low in self-confidence, not focused on what he could control, and fixated on potential failure.

Before the next meeting, we changed the imagery script in three important ways to focus on the aforementioned: self-confidence, perceived control, and approach goals.

So the situation was the same, but we added in reinforcements of Tim's ability to perform well, emphasized his readiness to take the putt, and got him to focus on the ball going into the hole. Similar to the quote from Curtis Strange, we encouraged Tim to focus on the positive aspects of his game and encouraged him to see himself making the shot. We repeated this on four separate occasions. We call this a challenge script. Take a look below (the highlighted parts are the good bits we added):

You are standing behind a putt looking for the line. It is your opponent's putt first. He has a similar length putt to you. He steps up confidently and makes the putt. Imagine how this makes you feel? (10secs).

It is now your turn, you need this putt for par. **You have made similar putts like this many times so feel confident in your ability to make the putt. Focus on these feelings of confidence** *(10secs).*

The putt is right to left down bank. You judge the line and **step up to the ball when you feel ready** *and take a few practice strokes.* **You know that if you strike the ball well it will go in. You feel confident and in control.** *You look once more at the hole and* **can imagine seeing the ball rolling into the hole; focus on these images** *(20secs).*

When we looked at Tim's cardiovascular data, we saw that his threat state had flipped to a challenge state when we gave him the challenge script. In contrast to before, Tim starting using the imagery so that his Cardiac Output increased and his Total Peripheral Resistance decreased from resting levels. By getting him to imagine approaching the putt with high resources, his body was now reacting in a challenge state.

More importantly, Tim started to perform more consistently, and no longer feared the dreaded 6 foot putt. His thoughts became clearer as he approached the shot and he started to consider the putt as an opportunity to show what he could do. His body responded to this change in mental approach by remaining composed and getting energy to his brain and body efficiently to produce a smooth putting action.

Happy days!

Dave the Rugby Player

The psychology of kicking is so important. You must visualize where the ball is going to go. Then you have to be able to trace that line from between the posts to the exact spot of the ball, and see that in your mind's eye when you go to kick the ball. Then I visualize the ball travelling along that path and imagine the sensation of how the ball is going to feel when it hits my foot for the perfect strike. The hard part is completing that action while standing in front of thousands of spectators with my heart thumping.[6]

Jonny Wilkinson, Rugby Player

Dave (not his real name) was a rugby player who wanted some help with his kicking. Not just kicking in general, but specifically kicking under pressure.

Pressure for Dave came after he took a kick that did not please him, such that his next kick would be more difficult as his confidence had been shaken. This was particularly problematic when he had to take kicks when the score was close and matches were tied, or his team were marginally in front or behind. It seemed that Dave's focus on the *consequences* of kicking poorly, and the fact that he had kicked poorly in the match already, interrupted his preparation for the kick, and therefore disrupted his performance.

After a couple of consultation sessions talking to Dave about these issues, we decided to see how his body responded to the thought of taking a pressured kick after a poor kick. So, as with Tim, we had Dave visualize the stressful situation while we recorded cardiovascular responses. Here is what we asked him to visualize:

You are about to take a kick having missed the previous two. (pause)

For the next minute or so, think about how you would feel in this situation as you have the ball in your hands, and wait for the referee to signal for you to place the ball for the kick. (pause)

Now imagine placing the ball and going through your normal pre-kick routine and taking the kick.

Dave's physiological response? A threat state. Obviously his shaken self-confidence was leading to a focus on failure, which affected his physiological response. We approached this situation differently than for Tim. Instead of changing the imagery, we worked with Dave to develop a pre-performance (or pre-kick) routine (more about routines in chapter 6).

This took a number of sessions where Dave would try some techniques then provide feedback on what he felt worked for him and what didn't. As the quote from Jonny Wilkinson illustrates, the ability to use visualization for this skill is vital, so it was important to include visualization in his routine. His final routine was this:

1. Place the ball.

2. Get into normal pre-kick start position and wait.

3. Breathe in for three seconds, then out for three seconds. On the exhale say the word "fluid" in your head (this is the kind of action he wants to produce as he kicks).

4. Then see the kick as you would perform it perfectly. Visualize running towards the ball in a particular rhythm (1, 2, 3) and feel the perfect contact on the ball.

5. As soon as you kick the ball in your visualization, begin your actual run up in the same way as imagined.

By reading between the lines you can see that the routine was about helping Dave to take *control* of the situation, and move past previous kicks to maintain *confidence*. Dave's physiological response, as with Tim, changed from a threat state to a challenge state the more he practiced this routine, and importantly his performance improved markedly with his kicking percentage rising from 50% to 80%. His routine gave him a reliable and consistent strategy to get into a challenge state and tip the balance in competition.

For both Tim and Dave, the ability to visualize was crucial in changing their threat state to a challenge state, and this skill forms a major part of the next chapter.

The Climb

Aside from our one-to-one consultancy work with athletes, we have also tested 'resources' in our lab using highly stressful sporting activities, or more accurately, in the face of a 10 metre climbing wall!

Imagine you are sitting, nice and relaxed, in a comfortable and quiet laboratory. Attached to your arm is a blood pressure cuff, and electrodes are placed on your wrists, ankles, and chest, monitoring your cardiovascular system.

After five minutes, a video appears on a screen in front of you. The video is shot in the first person and appears to be taking you into a sports facility. Coming into view is a huge climbing wall with an instructor waiting near it. A voice tells you that when you have finished watching the video, you will be required to climb the wall you see on the screen – the one that extends 10 metres upwards to the ceiling of the facility. As the camera waits at the bottom of the wall it pans upwards to give you a sense of the sheer height.

At this point, the voice tells you that because you have probably not done a task exactly like this before, you can't be confident in your ability to climb the wall, and that you do not have control over the skills needed to perform well. In fact, you should just try your best to *avoid falling off the wall*. As the video ends, the camera is now at the top of the wall looking over the facility; it dawns on you that, as the screen fades to black, you will now have to climb the wall.

In our lab, those who listened to the voice described above showed an increase in heart rate, showing that they were stressed-out about the wall. In turn, they reacted in a threat state. Their cardiovascular reactions showed that their body was reacting to the wall in a distressed way; a way that was inefficient and unhelpful.

In contrast, we also took another group of people and had them watch the exact same video, but this time, the voice told them that they had probably done similar tasks in the past and could therefore be confident that they could control their skills for the climb, and that they should focus on climbing as high as possible. Their reaction? A challenge state. Their body reacted to the wall in an efficient and helpful way.

The key difference in what the two sets of people heard was a matter of differing resources. People who were encouraged to have low self-confidence, low control, and to focus on avoidance goals reacted in a threat state. People who were encouraged to have high self-confidence, high control, and to focus on approach goals reacted in a challenge state.

Those encouraged to have high resources showed a challenge state when faced with climbing the wall.

Importantly, we did not help people into a challenge state by convincing them not to worry about the situation or by telling them that the task was easy and unimportant. This would have been unrealistic compared to real life. Rather, we simply helped those people to realize that they had the resources they needed to cope with the task, and this was sufficient to get them into a challenge state. Their bodies reacted according to the voice they heard – automatically.

Brief Summary

So, we know that enhancing resources leads to a challenge state, and that this can be done by visualizing the right things, and by adopting a consistent routine that tips the balance when needed. This is important because it means that there is a structure to follow and a method for getting into a challenge state. We also know that athletes in a challenge state perform to their potential.

In this short chapter, we have outlined some brief examples of how two specific athletes get into their challenge states, and how some simple instructions can help people into a challenge state in a highly stressful sporting activity. In the next three chapters you will learn many skills that we teach elite athletes who perform across a range of sports, which deal with each resource separately (self-confidence, control, and approach goals). You will learn how to increase each one effectively and in detail. You will learn how to do what Tim and Dave did. We will give you the tools you need to face tough, demanding situations in your sport, in the best possible way, by tipping the balance in your favour.

Happy tipping!

Most Important Point

Tipping the balance is about increasing and maintaining high levels of self-confidence, control, and approach goals. It is also about Thinking Smart so that the demands of your sport are kept in perspective.

---

[1] Waugh, S. (2005). *Out of my comfort zone: The autobiography*. London: Penguin Books.

[2] Moore, L. J., Vine, S. J., Wilson, M. R., & Freeman, P. (2012). The effect of challenge and threat states on performance: An examination of potential mechanisms. *Psychophysiology, 49*, (10), 1417-1425. doi: 10.1111/j.1469-8986.2012.01449.x

[3] Blascovich, J., Seery, M. D., Mugridge, C. A., Norris, R. K., & Weisbuch, M. (2004). Predicting athletic performance from cardiovascular indexes of challenge and threat. *Journal of Experimental Social Psychology, 40*, 683-688.

[4] Turner, M. J., Jones, M. V., Sheffield, D., Barker, J. B., & Coffee, P. (2014). Manipulating cardiovascular indices of challenge and threat states using resource appraisals. *International Journal of Psychophysiology, 94*, (1), 9-18.

[5] General sports motivational quotes (n. d.). *In mindtraining.net*. Retrieved May 21, 2014, from http://www.mindtraining.net/motivational-info/sports-champions-quotes/general-sports.php

[6] Jackson, J. (2003, October 5). How to be the best kicker in the world. *The Guardian*. Retrieved May 21, 2014, from http://www.theguardian.com/sport/2003/oct/05/rugbyworldcup2003.rugbyunion13

Chapter 5: Be Confident

Confidence is contagious;
so is a lack of confidence.[1]
Vince Lombardi, Two-time
Super Bowl Winning NFL Coach

"I very seldom have self-doubt. The thing I
always think about making a decision is not to
have any doubts about it...Why go to your bed
at night-time having doubts? Be clear. You
must have clarity in your decision-making.
What is right and what is wrong. To me it is
black and white. I try to erase doubts."[2]
Sir Alex Ferguson, Soccer Manager
who won 38 trophies, including
13 Premier League and 2 UEFA
Champions League titles

Kobe's 81

On January 22nd 2006, in a basketball game at the Staples Centre in Los Angeles - the LA Lakers took on and defeated the Toronto Raptors 122-104. In just under 42 minutes of on-court time, LA Lakers' shooting guard Kobe Bryant scored 81 points, a total that stands as the second-most prolific in league history, behind Wilt Chamberlain's 100-point game for the Philadelphia Warriors in March 1962.[3]

On that January day, Bryant glided around the court with speed and grace; everything he touched turned to gold. "I was just determined. I was just locked in, tuned into what was going on out there," he remarked about his performance. The Lakers' owner, Jerry West, said, "It's like a miracle unfolding in front of your eyes and you can't accept it... The easiest way to look at it is everybody remembers every 50-point game they ever saw. He had 55 in the second half." Even his opponents lauded Bryant's performance. Toronto's Chris Bosh remarked how, "We were just watching him shoot. He takes the type of shots where you don't think they're going in, but suddenly he's rolling, so he's kind of hard to stop. We tried three or four guys on him, but it seemed like nobody guarded him tonight."[4]

What can explain this phenomenal performance? Sure, being determined and obviously being highly skilled and incredibly fit are huge factors. But there are a lot of determined athletes who have high fitness and skill levels, and they don't produce performances like Bryant's. Bryant has spoken about what he experienced that night, and what stands out is his belief in his ability to score shot after shot.

"When you get in that zone, it's just a supreme confidence that you know it's going in. Things just slow down, everything just slows down and you just have supreme confidence. When that happens, you really do not try to focus on what's going on because you can lose it in a second. Everything becomes one noise, you don't hear this or that."[5]

From what Bryant says about his performance, his huge confidence levels led him to feeling "in that zone", a place that many athletes talk about in relation to peak performance. So what is this "supreme self-confidence" Bryant talks about? And can you experience it in your performances?

Put simply, self-confidence is the degree of certainty that you have in your ability to be successful in a certain situation. Self-confidence is the most powerful resource you will learn about in this book, because it so forcefully dictates how athletes perform. In this chapter we will first explore the value of self-confidence, and then move on to strategies that increase and maintain self-confidence for your sport performance.

I Prescribe Self-Confidence

If confidence could be packed into a pill it would be the most widely prescribed psychological pill on the market. Above and beyond the definition of self-confidence, you *know* what self-confidence is. It's been written about exhaustively in scientific and popular literature, and athletes attribute their success to it all the time. We know how important confidence is for success in sport at all levels of competition.

Research clearly, and consistently, demonstrates self-confidence to be one of the most important psychological factors relative to sport performance outcomes. Higher levels of confidence encourage athletes to cope with, and enjoy, performing under pressure, as well as offering the freedom to express their abilities and talents.

In addition, with increased confidence, athletes work harder, are persistent in the pursuit of their objectives, and set challenging goals - all of which contribute to superior performance. Of course, you can begin to understand the value and importance of having confidence if you want to maximize your sport performance. It follows that changes in your level of confidence influence the choices that you make, the execution of your skills, your emotions and behaviours, and how you perceive stressful situations such as competitions or vital training tests. It is a little wonder self-confidence is such a crucial component of The MAPP.

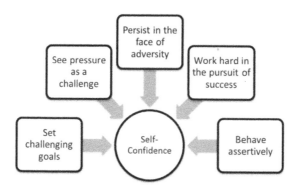

Is Your Confidence Robust?

The quest for any elite athlete is to have high levels of confidence, but more than this, the crux is to have *consistently* high confidence (regardless of the situation you are in).

Chapter 5

Contemporary sport psychology research has begun to explore individuals' robustness of self-confidence. That is, the stability of self-confidence when times are tough and obstacles are in athletes' paths.[6]

To illustrate, an athlete with robust self-confidence is an athlete who, in the face of failure or disappointment, continues to maintain their effort each day at training and in competition. Take a look at the two graphs at the end of this paragraph; they illustrate the self-confidence of two professional athletes over time. You can see that Mike's self-confidence takes a huge hit when he fails, and peaks when he succeeds. In contrast, Ian's confidence, while reducing slightly after failure, remains high no matter what. This is important as it means that Ian will be able to react to his failures more positively and therefore is likely to avoid subsequent poor performances in competition. You see, because self-confidence is so strongly linked to past performances, an inability to maintain high levels can lead to a vicious cycle of failure and ever-decreasing self-confidence. That is, for many athletes (like Mike) failure causes a significant decrease in self-confidence; which leads to subsequent failure; which in turn decreases self-confidence further; which then leads to even worse performance... and it goes on.

In this chapter you will learn not only how to *increase* your levels of self-confidence, but also how to *maintain* these high levels.

Mike's self-confidence over time

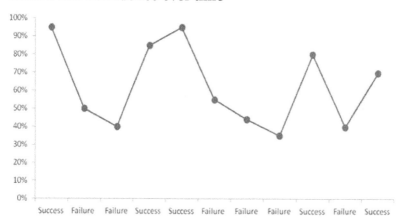

Ian's self-confidence over time

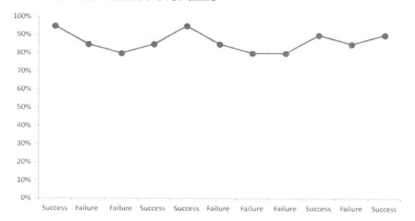

Self-Confidence vs. Arrogance

*Some people say that I have an attitude - maybe I do. But
I think that you have to. You have to
believe in yourself when no one else does - that
makes you a winner right there.[7]*

Venus Williams, Tennis Player

As demonstrated in the above Venus Williams quote, some people
may confuse your confidence for arrogance, and people may make
judgments about your attitude based on how confident you appear.
Managers and coaches often talk about wanting athletes who have
'the right attitude', but what does this actually mean? And how can
you make sure that your high self-confidence is not confused for
arrogance?

Having high levels of self-confidence is not the same as being
arrogant. Rather, confidence and arrogance are at two ends of a
continuum. To illustrate, at one end we have an athlete with high
confidence, who works hard, is very persistent, and who sets realistic
yet challenging targets for himself. At the other end, we have the
arrogant athlete, who may think he is too good to prepare for
important performances and hence reduces his effort levels, gives up
easily when training commitments become challenging, and sets
moderate career goals - all of which lead to moderate levels of overall
sport performance.

Robust confidence is central to dealing with pressure.

Stephen Hendry, snooker's World Number One for eight consecutive years between 1990 and 1998, famously recounted his complacency when approaching a World Championship Final match against Peter Ebdon. Hendry said that:

"I didn't think Peter could beat me. Simple as that. I did not go into the match with the right attitude. That is a terrible attitude to take into the final of the World Championships. But having beaten Ronnie [O'Sullivan] in the semi, I thought I just had to turn up at the final to win. At times I wasn't even there. Even when it got to 17-17, I still thought I was going to win. When I didn't I was shocked. It was a painful mistake to make."[8]

John Lennon, of The Beatles, notoriously said, "If being an egomaniac means I believe in what I do and in my art or music, then in that respect you can call me that... I believe in what I do, and I'll say it."[9] In other words, sometimes high self-confidence may *appear* arrogant to other people, but that's *their* problem not yours!

The important thing to remember is that high self-confidence is different to arrogance in many ways. Believing in yourself is about three main things:

1. The ability to enhance your levels of confidence

2. Maintaining those levels no matter what

3. Making sure you don't fall into the trap of being over-confident, or arrogant

---

Confidence and arrogance are at opposite ends - confident people work hard, are persistent and stay on task. Arrogant people do none of these things.

A Place to Start

Let's do a little self-awareness test so that you can understand where you are, now, with your self-confidence. Respond to the four statements below (based on a measure by Dr. Stuart Beattie and colleagues)[10]. Once you have done this, work out your average score (add all scores together and divide by 4).

To what extent do you agree that…

	Completely Disagree	Somewhat Disagree	Neither Agree nor Disagree	Somewhat Agree	Completely Agree
Failing has a huge effect on my confidence	1	2	3	4	5
My confidence goes up and down (fluctuates) a lot	1	2	3	4	5
When things don't go to plan, my confidence hits rock bottom	1	2	3	4	5
My confidence depends on success and failure	1	2	3	4	5

If your average score is below 2, then your confidence is quite robust. It may not be as high as it could be, but it remains pretty stable regardless of success and failure. If your score is between 2 and 4, then most of the time your confidence is stable, but sometimes failure really brings it down, and success boosts it a lot. If your score is above 4, then your confidence is really affected by success and failure and, in essence, your self-belief is at the beck and call of your performance. You will feel 100% confident one day, and 0% the next. This can be exhausting, but fear not, read on.

Knowledge is Power

How much do we really know about how to increase and maintain confidence?

As with everything else in this book, there is no big secret, no magical spell or recipe. Hopefully, what you are starting to realize is that the power of the human mind is the most important weapon you will ever possess when it comes to dealing with pressured and tough situations in your sport. Specifically, the mental ability to change the way you see the world, and importantly yourself, is one of the most important skills you will learn over the course of this book.

Really, self-confidence is about perception and is rarely based on reality. For example, we know from research that confidence is a hugely changeable mental state, and we can manipulate confidence very well using false feedback.

False feedback involves telling someone they have performed poorly regardless of their actual objective performance. So let's take Ian from our self-confidence graphs earlier in the chapter and put him through his paces on a couple of hand-eye coordination tests. We tell him that he is in a competition and that his performance will be compared to others and ranked on a league table. On the first hand-eye coordination trial, Ian performs excellently, but he has no idea how his competitors have performed. So, we lie to Ian and falsely tell him that he has performed poorly and that he is currently one of the five worst performers to complete the test. We give Ian another shot at success. But when Ian completes his second trial, he performs much worse than he did in his first trial. By telling him he is poor at the task, his self-confidence takes a blow, regardless of his actual performance, thus ruining his subsequent performance.

This has huge implications. This means that the feedback you receive, and indeed deliver, can determine yours and others' self-confidence. Now, of course, you can't control how somebody gives you feedback, or what they say to you (more on this in the next chapter) but you can control the feedback you give to yourself and can *choose* the words to help tip the balance in your favour.

On the back of a poor performance, you have the opportunity to maintain your self-confidence by focusing on the pleasing aspects of your performance. On the back of a successful performance, you can make a concerted effort to reflect on all of the great things you did to achieve your goal. Don't be afraid to pat yourself on the back. What you say to yourself is one of the best ways to change self-confidence. Sport psychologists call this "self-talk" and this is just one of many well-supported strategies that can help you to maintain your self-confidence (we will cover self-talk, in detail, in the next chapter).

For the rest of this chapter, we want to focus on a very powerful confidence-boosting strategy called visualization, and we will also signpost other useful techniques along the way. The underlying principle of what you will learn from here, is that you can choose to feel confident whenever you want. *You* are in the driver's seat.

Being confident is a choice - choose to believe in yourself.

Remember the Time...

For a moment, pause and reflect on your competitive experiences. Think of a time when you were sure you would perform well: you were in control, certain of success even if things got tough. You had an unshakeable belief in your abilities - so sure of yourself. You felt like you were on autopilot, able to perform effortlessly.

How did it feel? What happened to your performance? Dwell on this fabulous experience for a while.

Now snap out of it. We don't want you to get big-headed!

The ability to look back at past experiences when you felt highly confident, and when you performed well, is crucial. Dr. Albert Bandura, a psychologist rightly considered the leading authority on self-confidence related topics, proposed that self-confidence is influenced by a number of sources of information; and *the most powerful* source is past accomplishments. Further, if you can picture an accomplishment so well in your head that it feels for a moment like you were *reliving* it, then the power of this memory is magnified.

This incredible ability to think back to moments of glory and relive those feelings can be harnessed using visualization. Let's focus explicitly on this powerful and learnable skill.

See It, Feel It, Do It

Visualization, also known as imagery or mental rehearsal, is a fascinating mental ability. There is good evidence that using visualization to specifically prepare for upcoming sport performances helps to enhance self-confidence and consequent performance.

By realistically imagining yourself in that cup final and seeing yourself perform well - with control and composure despite being uncomfortable - you can more confidently approach an actual cup final in the same way: with control and composure. Visualization is *not* about wishful thinking. It's about mentally rehearsing your best performance before you do it.

The underlying reasons for the effectiveness of visualization are still under debate. But broadly, by imagining a competitive situation as realistically as you can (including sights, sounds, and feelings), the brain starts to respond in a similar way to if you were *actually* facing that competitive situation. If you are able to 'see' what you would see in an actual competition, 'hear' the same sounds, and 'feel' the same things, then you can recreate the mental and physical responses that are experienced in actual competition. So the feelings of control and composure will feel very real and will boost your confidence for that specific situation. In other words, if you want to be confident, controlled and composed under pressure, then imagine being so! Think of it as creating a mental blueprint of how to succeed when it matters most - a dress rehearsal for the opening night.

"Part of my preparation is I go and ask the kit man what colour we're wearing — if it's red top, white shorts, white socks or black socks. Then I lie in bed the night before the game and visualize myself scoring goals or doing well. You're trying to put yourself in that moment and trying to prepare yourself, to have a 'memory' before the game. I don't know if you'd call it visualizing or dreaming, but I've

always done it, my whole life… When I was younger, I used to visualize myself scoring wonder goals, stuff like that. From 30 yards out, dribbling through teams. You used to visualize yourself doing all that, and when you're playing professionally, you realize it's important for your preparation."[1] - Wayne Rooney, Manchester United and England Footballer.

"I started my automatic default mechanism of visualizing myself running the race… I would hear the gun go off in my head, and start going through my paces. Then I'd visualize the whole thing again… I focused on running the perfect race in my head."[2] - Michael Johnson, Track Athlete

---

*Imagery enhances confidence and athletes'
ability to deal with pressure.*

Many elite athletes report using visualization. This makes sense given how research demonstrates that athletes with high confidence maintain images of successful performances, and that visualization can have a positive impact on self-confidence. One of the most famous advocates of visualization is Jack Nicklaus, a golfer who won 18 career major championships. Below, Nicklaus describes his pre-shot routine:

"I never hit a shot, not even in practice, without having a very sharp, in-focus picture of it in my head. It's like a color movie. First, I see the ball where I want it to finish, nice and white and sitting up high on the bright green grass. Then the scene quickly changes and I "see" the ball going there: its path, trajectory, and shape, even its behavior on landing. Then there's sort of a fade-out, and the next scene shows me making the kind of swing that will turn the previous images into reality. Only at the end of this short, private, Hollywood spectacular do I select a club and step up to the ball."[3]

Notice how detailed Nicklaus makes the visualization. The more detailed and realistic the imagery, the more effective it will be for creating and maintaining confidence. Think of it as creating a mental blueprint for successful performance. The more detailed and accurate you make the blueprint, the more likely you can recreate that success in actual performance. In fact, many athletes talk about this idea of developing and strengthening a mental blueprint. By imagining what you want to do before you do it, you are mapping out the details so that, when it is time to perform, you know exactly what you need to do. By witnessing yourself performing perfectly, you are building and strengthening the blueprint for success. More importantly, if you are able to very realistically see yourself succeed, you can be sure of your ability to re-create that success in an actual performance.

Use imagery to create a mental blueprint for success.

So how do you begin to build this mental blueprint? Let's find out how you can adopt simple strategies to develop your imagery ability, and make your visions become reality.

My Visualization Ammunition

Visualization can be used in lots of different ways so it is important to use it in the right way to increase self-confidence. One of the ways we encourage athletes to develop their imagery for performance is to stock up on "Visualization Ammunition".

Practically, this is a mental (in your head) or physical (written down) database of key past experiences and achievements that can be used flexibly within your visualization. Have a go at stocking up your ammunition by recalling times when you felt highly proficient and times when you experienced optimal performance in your sport. Really try to think back to those moments of success and dwell on them. This may be difficult for some because we often don't spend time dwelling on the good things that happen to us. Write these experiences down.

One really effective way to develop your ammunition is to get into the habit of *reflecting* on your experiences. This can be formal or informal, but importantly, it's about reflecting in a way that recognizes all the good stuff you do when you compete and train, while keeping an eye out for key developmental aspects. Buy a notebook, and write down your personal ammunition. Alternatively, create a new document on your computer, smartphone, or other electronic device and type out your ammunition. Refer to these resources regularly!

As an example of self-reflection, here are the thoughts of an elite cricketer we worked with:

Two things that went well today...

1. My defensive batting was superb today as I was able to stay in for a long period of time and really started to frustrate the bowlers.

2. I was able to hold my nerve when things got really pressured midway through the match. Even though I was under immense pressure I was able to maintain composure and bat through the tough situation.

One thing I want to improve, and how it will be addressed...

I could have scored more runs if I was more aggressive in my shots and if I had a little more courage at key moments. I will practice my scoring under pressure with a very fast bowling machine.

This reflection was completed in the evening after a match and you will notice a few key things about it. First is that all of the events in the reflection are controllable by the athlete (more on this in the next chapter), which means that he can be in charge of improvements. Second, it's all about positivity. It's about recognizing best practice and improving. Doing this frequently will help you to develop a bank of moments in which you have done well, and which can therefore feed directly into your visualization ammunition.

Another way to develop your ammunition is to self-model. This doesn't mean putting on your best designer clothes and hitting the catwalk! Self-modelling involves using yourself as a source of confidence, but more specifically, actually seeing yourself perform well. The most obvious way you can do this is to video record yourself performing in training or in competition. Indeed, many of you will already record your performances, or have access to match performances for your team, that you can use. You subsequently view the recording and engage in the reflection we touched on earlier. You can actually see the strengths that you have - onscreen - and can begin to act on the areas requiring development. This strategy can obviously be tricky to put into practice but it is really effective at giving you detailed artillery for you visualization ammunition.

In fact, in the elite sporting environment, performance analysis is a big part of maximizing potential as a performer. Most elite teams have a video-analyst and part of their job is to make performance footage available to athletes in the team. At the 2014 Sochi Winter Olympics, Scott Novack (director of high performance for the U.S. Bobsled and Skeleton Federation) talked about the team's use of video analysis. Novack remarked that, "We only get a handful of (practice) runs, specifically six runs of official training, which is why video analysis becomes crucial."[14] Novack video records the team's runs at different curves so that strengths and areas for development can be instantly analysed by the coach. Novack went on to say: "In between runs, we were reviewing the video and that helped contribute to the two Olympic medals that we were able to get in Vancouver," (the team won gold for their four-man bobsled team, and bronze for the two-woman bobsled team).

So, video record or access your performance footage and start to understand where your specific strength areas are, and where you may want to develop things. The main thing here is to really focus on what you do well so that you can add to your visualization ammunition!

*Reflection is a key aspect of your confidence
ammo - reflection builds confidence.*

When you have stocked up on ammunition, you can then decide how you would like to structure your imagery. We typically use three main strategies with elite athletes who want to use imagery to enhance confidence for an upcoming high-pressure competition:

1. Highlight reel

2. Real-time best performance

3. Smart imagery

1. Highlight Reel

*A good athlete always mentally replays a competition over
and over, even in victory, to see what might be done to
improve the performance the next time.*[15]

Frank Shorter, Track Athlete

This is really all about creating a cinematic experience for yourself in your mind where you experience various best performances back-to-back. Similar to a replay of a sporting event on TV, you include only the most important aspects, and crucially, only the aspects when you performed in ways that you want to recreate in the future (e.g., good performances).

This strategy can be a powerful booster of self-confidence as it serves as evidence that you have achieved optimal performance many times in the past and can therefore do it again. With one soccer athlete, we encouraged him to create a "Match of the Day" television scenario in his head. This involved Gary Lineker (the show's presenter) introducing the highlights, after which the athlete would witness and experience himself making perfect passes, scoring goals, making important tackles, winning headers, etc. This was useful when he was traveling to competitions. It is very easy to create a highlight reel for yourself. Use your visualization ammunition to create a greatest hits montage of you at your best!

2. Real-time Best Performance

Dreaming means 'rehearsing' what you see, playing it over and over in your mind until it becomes as real to you as your life right now.[16]

Emmitt Smith, NFL Footballer

As the title suggests, this strategy requires you to think of one specific situation when your performance was at its best and success was attained. So it's not about visualizing lots of situations like in the highlight reel, but more about focusing on one great performance.

When you can think back to the event and recall a lot of specifics, write a narrative for the situation with as much detail as possible (recalling thoughts, feelings, and behaviours). Practice this imagery script until you can imagine the scenario either with your eyes open or closed, without the need of a script. Practically, you can use this strategy whenever you feel it appropriate to boost your confidence – typically in the lead up to performances.

For example, athletes may engage in imagery prior to an important competition or training session, or in the days leading up to an important tournament. The real strength of this type of imagery is that it taps into the most important source of confidence (as outlined previously): *past experiences*. The specific, real-time elements will help your brain to build that blueprint of best performance that we discussed earlier, boosting confidence and making success more likely.

If you are feeling adventurous, we suggest you record this script onto your mp3 player, phone or tablet for use during quiet times, or on your journey to a competition venue. The better you embed this technique into your way of thinking, the better you will become at visualizing and the better it will be for performance.

Below is an example of a cricketer's best performance imagery script:

Recall the confidence and belief you have as you stand at the crease staring at the bowler as he runs... recall the clarity with which you see the ball leave the bowler's hand and make its way down the wicket... feel yourself quickly move into position as you quickly, decisively and confidently judge the line and length... feel the solid contact your bat makes with the ball on the half volley... hear the sound of the ball coming out of the middle... see the ball disappear quickly and accurately through the covers and over the boundary rope... feel yourself punch the air with joy after overcoming this difficult situation... recall the pleasure and feelings of knowing that you've just been successful... recall the feeling and thoughts of knowing that you are good... recall the feelings of excitement, pleasure and confidence as you walk into the pavilion and analyse what you have just achieved.

Here is a soccer goalkeeping example. The goalkeeper developed this based on a past performance:

Recall the confidence you feel as you spin the ball in your hands to find the ball logo...feel the weight of the ball...you place the ball down with the logo facing you on a rise in the turf....notice the texture of the ball as you place it down... you take 6 steps back...now notice how the texture changes as you get further away from the ball...you take two steps to the side...feel the intensity as you stare at the ball with your head down...envisage the area that you are about to strike...you imagine a precise chain of a events that will follow the kick.....it feels right...you know it will be a great kick....scan round the pitch and see the area you will land the ball in...approach the ball...feel the energy running through your body as you approach the ball...you plant your non-kicking foot next to the ball perfectly and swing your kicking foot...you ping the ball on its sweet spot...and the ball flies from your foot...you know it's a perfect kick...as your head comes up you see the ball fly past the half way line toward your target, just as you imagine...you follow the ball out walking toward the halfway line...the ball is driving like an arrow past midfield right to your target area...you know that you have performed a great kick...see the ball drop to your target and be elated at your amazing kick...recall the feeling of pleasure, confidence and pride at your kick for a few moments.

3. Smart Imagery

Another effective type of imagery involves imagining yourself effectively coping with, and mastering, challenging situations in your sport. In particular, this includes visualizing yourself in highly pressured situations whilst holding Smart Thoughts as discussed in chapter 3.

Try this. Take a few slow breaths and relax. Now visualize being in a really uncomfortable pressured competition you have experienced, or one that is coming up in your season. Be very detailed in your visualization (remember, the more senses you can recreate, the better). Let the situation happen in your mind. Feel the emotions; imagine this situation until the emotions are as unbearable as you can get them. Keep doing this for a minute or so.[17]

Now, change your emotions from unbearable to unpleasant *but do not change the situation*. Change from highly anxious to ready. From worried to confident. Take your time to do this properly. You can do it - you are the one in control here. Change your emotions without changing the situation. Don't change any factual information about the event.

How did you do it? You changed what you thought about the situation, not the situation itself. That is, you changed B, not A, to make C more beneficial for performance. It's the thinking that causes emotion. Now try it again, and this time go into the visualization with the mantra "I really want to do well in this competition, but it won't kill me if I don't!" and/or "Failure to perform well here will not make me a complete failure." You may find that you are more able to change how you feel by using these Smart Thinking statements.

Importantly, you may still feel stressed. But remember this is good! Stress can be really helpful for your performance if you are in a challenge state (see The MAPP). The main point here is that imagery can be used to practice your Smart Thinking so that, when faced with a real competition, Thinking Smart will be your default reaction, helping to control emotions and retain self-confidence.

Practice Makes Permanent

For imagery to be effective - practice is vital.

The key aspect to any mental skill is to practice, and imagery is no different. Indeed, we advise practicing the imagery script daily, for 10 minutes, for at least two weeks before it is integrated into your training and performance routines. In other words, do not only use visualization right before that all important match or race, use it consistently in the lead up to the event, in the days and weeks prior.

A man is but the product of his thoughts. What he thinks, he becomes.[18]

Mohandas K. Gandhi, Politician

It's Not All About You

Thus far, to enhance and maintain self-confidence we have stressed the importance of mentally rehearsing success and seeing yourself performing well in tough situations in your mind's eye. But confidence can also be derived through observing the performances and behaviours of other athletes, for example your teammates, and noting the consequences of their actions.

In turn, a new athlete to the team seeing a more established member deal effectively with a pressure situation can increase their own levels of self-confidence through the adoption of a "If they can do it, so can I" approach.

Observing repeated demonstrations by experienced and skilled athletes can provide information to others on how to perform, as well as provide information that the skills needed for the task can be learnt and that success is attainable.

I used to imagine what it would be like to do what Jim Brown was doing. I used to imagine what it would be like to be like a Tony Dorsett. I used to imagine what it would be like to be like a Walter Payton. I was imagining Emmitt Smith doing exactly what they were doing.[19]

Emmitt Smith, NFL Footballer

In a similar way, you can also gain confidence through what people say to you. Verbal instruction can be provided by captains, managers, sport science staff, teammates, and partners. For example, before a difficult competition (e.g., championship game) a partner or teammate may remind you that you have done well in tough competitions in the past and can, therefore, do well in the upcoming game. Indeed, this type of external verbal instruction can be motivational too, and can help you to focus your thoughts.

Further, if you are a captain or leader in your team you can influence the thoughts and feelings of others by using verbal instruction that enhances confidence. One of the activities we conduct with athletes is to pair them up with a teammate and get them to provide feedback to each other on "what you can do to help me perform better". So athlete A will ask athlete B to do something differently or maintain a behaviour because it helps them perform well. By far the most common suggestion that comes from this task is that athletes want to be encouraged more, and that this encouragement is needed not only when they are down, but also when they are up. Even when people are feeling good about themselves, they still value that verbal encouragement. If you are in a leadership role, think about how you can increase the confidence of your team by getting them to think about past success, but also by leading in a confident manner – lead by example.

Confidence is influenced by what we say
to ourselves and what others say to us.

The capacity for this type of information to influence confidence depends on the prestige, credibility, expertise, and trustworthiness of the person(s) providing the instruction. So, ensure that you have a supportive network of individuals that you respect and trust. By talking to these significant others about your challenges you may find that they are able to provide you with an extra source of confidence that can further tip the balance in your favour.

Body Language

If you are not the best, then
pretend you are.[20]

Muhammad Ali, Boxer

Everything we have said in this chapter is about increasing your feelings of self-confidence and maintaining this state of belief. But in some situations not only do you want to feel confident, you want to look confident too. Across competitive and training situations people will make judgments about how confident an athlete is on the basis of their body language (e.g., how they walk into a competition arena, how they behave, and cope with pressure). And on the back of this judgment, people arrive very rapidly at a conclusion about your credibility.

Research suggests that athletes who *look confident* are perceived as more likely to be successful. One research study showed that table tennis and tennis athletes who approached a serve with positive body language (stand and walk erect, shoulders back and chest out, head up, chin level with the ground, their eyes looking directly at the camera (the opponent) for prolonged periods of time), were perceived as: prepared, confident, focused, relaxed, assertive, aggressive, competitive, experienced, fit, and of a higher ability than the opposition.[21, 22]

In contrast, athletes who approached the serve with negative body language (hunched posture, head and chin held down, with eyes looking down or briefly glancing at the opponent) were perceived as: under-prepared, lethargic, not confident, not focused, tense, not assertive, not aggressive, not competitive, a novice, unfit, and of a lower ability.

Most strikingly, participants felt that they would have a much greater chance of defeating the athletes with negative body language than the athletes with positive body language. Even before the contest begins, athletes were predicting their own demise.

As I passed Shahid Afridi on the way out,
he said I looked positive. I thought that's
what you need to look like. That's what
the people I talk to have been saying, 'stop walking
out like a schoolboy and walk out, chest out, like
you mean business. With a presence.'[23]

Ian Bell, Cricketer
after his 115
in Faisalabad against Pakistan

So what does all this mean? An individual who walks into a competition venue with their head held high - walking tall - displays confidence and composure. In contrast, an athlete who walks in with their head held low, hunched posture, demonstrates anxiety and concern. Further, the message you send to others with your behaviour influences the view they take of your skills and abilities. Would you trust a soccer athlete to take a penalty in a shoot-out if they looked unsure of themselves, nervous and panicky, unable to maintain composure? That athlete might be brilliant, but their lack of confident behaviour is sending out the opposite message. After all, if they were so brilliant, and they were able to take accurate penalties, why aren't they more confident about it?

In our work with elite athletes we encourage them to pick a role model, or someone who they think has strong, positive body language, and simply adopt that person's body language. We want them to act confidently even if, inside, they may not feel 100% sure of themselves. The real benefit of this approach is that it will influence the perceptions of others, so that on approach to that final race or penalty kick you are viewed as a confident, assertive, and composed professional. Your leadership is viewed as authoritative and powerful. Scouts see you as a composed, enthusiastic, and reliable on the field of play; not a nervous, panicky, liability.

Football means a hell of a lot to me. It was like an acting job, I used to feel that when I drove up to Old Trafford I would turn into this kind of mean machine.[24]

Roy Keane, Footballer

Over time, by acting like a confident athlete, you will also start to think and feel like a confident athlete. Psychologists call this 'embodied cognition'[25] and it simply means that not only do you need to think confidently in order to act confidently, you need to act confidently in order to think confidently.

Many scientific studies have shown that by adopting particular behaviours, thoughts can be altered and manipulated. For example, in one study people were asked to adopt different facial expressions and postures while recalling pleasant or unpleasant autobiographical memories. It was found that when people smiled and adopted an erect posture, the retrieval of pleasant memories was faster than for the retrieval of unpleasant memories. So acting positively helped the participants to think positively.

If we relate this to self-confidence, we can start to understand just how multidimensional the quote from Muhammad Ali, at the start of this section, really is. Social psychologist Amy Cuddy has found that job candidates adopting a confident body posture were more likely to be hired than those who adopted a non-confident body posture.[26] This could be due to various factors. Biologically, confident body language increases testosterone (linked to dominance) and decreases cortisol (linked to a threat state - see chapter 2) therefore physiologically the body is reacting positively to the situation.

Think of it like this. By acting confidently, your body is telling your brain that you are confident, dominant, and ready to perform. The brain receives that message and says "hmm, I must be confident, because I only behave like this when I am confident." This is an important ingredient in performing when it matters most, so here's a synthesis of what confident body language is:

- Stand and walk erect

- Sit up straight when waiting to perform

- Shoulders back and chest out

- Head up

- Chin parallel with the ground

- Maintain eye contact with opponents and teammates

- Smile! Confident people are happy because they know they can succeed.

Acting like a confident performer will boost your inner confidence. Be sure to pick a role model and copy them.

So, as you can see, by choosing the right thoughts (positive visualization) and adopting the right behaviour (body language) you can ensure that you are mentally and physically in the right state to perform at your best. Try it today. Stand in front of a mirror and take on the role of a confident athlete. Then take on the role of a non-confident athlete. Which one makes you look more unbeatable, and importantly which one helps you feel more self-assured?

An Ode to Self-Doubt

Much of chapter 5 has waxed lyrical about the perks of self-confidence. But remember – arrogance is not the same as confidence. If you are too confident, this can lead to complacency and withdrawn effort. If you 'know' you will win, then why put in maximal effort? This attitude can lead to unexpected failure.

Research has shown that a little self-doubt is a good thing.[27] The popular belief is that the more self-confidence you have the better your performance, but there is a point at which this confidence becomes arrogance, and performance can actually be harmed. This supports what athletes say about self-doubt giving them an extra edge in their performance. For example, going back to Kobe Bryant: "I have self-doubt. I have insecurity. I have fear of failure. I have nights when I show up at the arena and I'm like, 'My back hurts, my feet hurt, my knees hurt. I don't have it. I just want to chill.' We all have self-doubt. You don't deny it, but you also don't capitulate to it. You embrace it."[28]

So don't worry too much if you have a little self-doubt from time to time. Look back to Ian's self-confidence graph earlier in the chapter – some dips in self-confidence occur – but your job is make sure these dips are minor and are followed by balanced reflections on what you do well. The important thing is to make sure you feel that you can express yourself fully and have the ability to succeed, not that success is certain. The key is awareness and being able to recognize when this self-doubt becomes a problem for your sport performance.

Brief Summary

Believe you can and you're halfway there.[29]

Theodore Roosevelt, Politician

Confidence is one of the most important psychological factors related to effective sport performance. As we have seen in this chapter, confidence is derived from many sources of internal (ourselves) and external (our environment) information. In addition, increased confidence is associated with numerous benefits, including increased effort, persistence, and performance.

In sport your attitude will also impact upon the way you and your team works. Teams with the 'right' attitude are generally seen to apply themselves effectively to whatever is asked of them, and give 100% in training and competitions. These positive athletes are willing to work hard and always *believe* that they can do it. So, it makes sense that positive people are more likely to be successful, because deep down they think they will be. They will always look to find a solution to a problem, even in the most difficult situations, and will persist in the face of setbacks.

Luke: I can't believe it.

Yoda: That is why you fail.[30]

Star Wars

Most Important Point

Self-confidence can be enhanced and maintained by reflecting on past performances in a balanced way, adopting positive thoughts, and behaving confidently.

[1] Quoteswave. (2013, June12). *Vince Lombardi quotes* [Video file]. Retrieved May 21, 2014, from http://www.youtube.com/watch?v=Kya3FiExzlE

[2] Soderling, R. (2012). Sir Alex Ferguson says self belief is the secret of his success. *In sportqa.com*. Retrieved May 21, 2014, from http://www.sportqa.com/Sir-Alex-Ferguson-says-self-belief-is-the-secret-of-his-success-a14585

[3] Martin, J. (2014, January 22). Re-Examining Kobe Bryant's 81-Point Game Through a 2014 Lens. *Bleacher Report*. Retrieved May 21, 2014, from

http://bleacherreport.com/articles/1931983-re-examining-kobe-bryants-81-point-game-through-a-2014-lens

[4] Kobe's 81-point game second only to Wilt. (2006, January 22). *ESPN NBA*. Retrieved May 21, 2014, from http://scores.espn.go.com/nba/recap?gameId=260122013

[5] Woodyard, E. (2014, January 22). Best Individual Performance of the Decade: Kobe Bryant's 81 Point Game! *Flintstones*. Retrieved May 21, 2014, from http://eric32woodyard.wordpress.com/2009/12/30/best-individual-performance-of-the-decade-kobe-bryants-81-point-game/

[6] Beattie, S., Hardy, L., Savage, J., Woodman, T., & Callow, N. (2011). Development and validation of a trait measure of robustness of self-confidence. *Psychology of Sport and Exercise, 12*, 2, 184–191.

[7] Venus Williams Quotes. (n. d.). *In thinkexist.com*. Retrieved May 21, 2014, from http://thinkexist.com/quotation/some_people_say_that_i_have_an_attitude-maybe_i/250648.html

[8] Harris, N. (2003, April 16). Snooker: Hendry determined to make amends for final aberration. *The Independent*. Retrieved May 21, 2014, from http://www.independent.co.uk/sport/general/snooker-hendry-determined-to-make-amends-for-final-aberration-115313.html

[9] Pulsifer, C. (2014, January 22). John Lennon Quotes. *In Wow4U.com*. Retrieved May 21, 2014, from http://www.wow4u.com/johnlennonquotes/

[10] Beattie, S., Hardy, L., Savage, J., Woodman, T., & Callow, N. (2011). Development and validation of a trait measure of robustness of self-confidence. *Psychology of Sport and Exercise, 12*, 2, 184–191.

[11] Winner, D. (2012, May 16). Beautiful game. Beautiful mind. *ESPN The Magazine*. Retrieved May 21, 2014, from http://www.espnfc.com/euro2012/en/news/1071240/beautiful-game-beautiful-mind-.html

[12] Johnson, M. (2012). *Gold rush*. London: Harper Collins.

[13] Nicklaus, J., & Bowden, K. (1974). *Golf my way*. Simon & Schuster.

[14] Baker, N. (2014, February 17 For Olympic athletes, tools for medal chase include video analysis apps. *Reuters*. Retrieved May 21, 2014, from

http://www.reuters.com/article/2014/02/17/apps-olympics-idUSL2N0LK0CO20140217

[15] Imagery. (n. d.). *In Sport Psychology Quotes*. Retrieved May 21, 2014, from https://sportpsychquotes.wordpress.com/tag/imagery/

[16] Imagery. (n. d.). *In Sport Psychology Quotes*. Retrieved May 21, 2014, from https://sportpsychquotes.wordpress.com/tag/imagery/

[17] Rational Emotive Imagery. (n. d.). *In 25-7 help*. Retrieved May 21, 2014, from http://www.24-7help.com/about_rebt/REI.php

[18] Writecreativelyblog (2012, December, 17). Poems. *Section poems*. Retrieved May 21, 2014, from http://sectionpoems.wordpress.com/2012/12/17/mahatma-gandhi-a-man-is-but-the-product-of-his-thoughts-what-he-thinks-he-becomes/

[19] Imagery. (n. d.). *In Sport Psychology Quotes*. Retrieved May 21, 2014, from https://sportpsychquotes.wordpress.com/tag/imagery/

[20] Muhammad Ali Quotes (n. d.). In *iheartinspiration.com*. Retrieved May 21, 2014, from http://iheartinspiration.com/quotes/to-be-a-great-champion-you-must-believe-you-are-the-best/

[21] Greenlees, I., Buscombe, R., Thelwell, Richard, Holder, T. and Rimmer, M. (2005) Impact of opponents' clothing and body language on impression formation and outcome expectations. *Journal of Sport & Exercise Psychology*, *27*, 1, 39-52.

[22] Greenlees, I.A., Bradley, A., Holder, T.P., & Thelwell, R.C. (2005). The impact of two forms of opponents' non-verbal communication on impression formation and outcome expectations. *Psychology of Sport & Exercise*, *6*, 103-115.

[23] Brenkley, S. (2005, November 27). The 10-minute fix that put Bell in full swing once more. *The Independent*. Retrieved May 21, 2014, from http://www.independent.co.uk/sport/cricket/the-10minute-fix-that-put-bell-in-full-swing-once-more-329548.html

[24] Walker, M. (2006, August 30). Keane checks in with apologies but no regrets. *The Guardian*. Retrieved May 21, 2014, from http://www.theguardian.com/football/2006/aug/30/newsstory.sport6

[25] McNerney, S. (2011, November 4). A Brief Guide to Embodied Cognition: Why You Are Not Your Brain. *Scientific American*. Retrieved May 21, 2014, from http://blogs.scientificamerican.com/guest-

blog/2011/11/04/a-brief-guide-to-embodied-cognition-why-you-are-not-your-brain/

[26] TED. (2012, October 1). *Amy Cuddy: Your body language shapes who you are* [Video file]. Retrieved May 21, 2014, from http://www.youtube.com/watch?v=Ks-_Mh1QhMc

[27] Woodman, T., Akehurstb, S., Hardy, L., & Beattie, S. (2010). Self-confidence and performance: A little self-doubt helps. *Psychology of Sport and Exercise, 11*, 6, 467–470.

[28] Self-doubt quotes. (n. d.). *In brainyquote.com.* Retrieved May 21, 2014, from http://www.brainyquote.com/quotes/keywords/self-doubt.html#RFHHvqIVtu7Ft8Zj.99

[29] Theodore Roosevelt quotes. (n. d.). *In brainyquote.com.* Retrieved May 21, 2014, from http://www.brainyquote.com/quotes/quotes/t/theodorero380703.html

[30] Yoda quotes. (n. d.). *In yodaquotes.net.* Retrieved May 21, 2014, from http://www.yodaquotes.net/luke-i-cant-believe-it-yoda-that-is-why-you-fail/

Chapter 6: Be In Control

 The best years of your life are the ones in which you decide your problems are your own. You do not blame them on your mother, the ecology, or the president. You realize that you control your own destiny.[1]

Dr. Albert Ellis (September 27, 1913 – July 24, 2007), one of the originators of cognitive-behavioural therapy, considered as the second most influential psychotherapist in history (after Carl Rogers)

Where were you in 2008, when the greatest tennis match of all time was taking place at Wimbledon? If (like us) you were transfixed in front of the TV watching Roger Federer and Rafa Nadal produce some of the best tennis ever seen, then you may remember some of the circumstances that contributed to this match being particularly memorable.

After a 35-minute rain delay Nadal started well, saving three break points and taking the first set. Federer got back into the match and took a 4-1 lead in the second set, but Nadal - undeterred - won five straight games to take a two-set lead.

At this point, dark clouds began to gather above Centre Court. In the third set Federer looked like he may capitulate, but managed to step up and take a 5-4 lead. Then rain stopped play!

After an 80 minute rain delay, Federer resumed with renewed vigour and took the third set with an emphatic ace. The fourth went to a tie break, during which some of the most amazing tennis you will ever see occurred. This classic tie-break saw Federer recover from 5-2 down to miss a set point with an inaccurate forehand. At 7-6 Nadal lost a championship point to a winning serve from Federer, who then saved a second match point with an awesome backhand winner.

Federer served a winner to take the match into a fifth set.

Then, more rain!

The score was now two sets all, and most people thought the match would have to be continued the following day. It was almost 8pm. But the rain passed in half an hour and the players returned to the court.

At this point, the light was dull. Compared to the quality of light at the start of the match, this was a huge challenge for the players to overcome. But the final set was unbelievable.

Federer earned a break point in game eight, Nadal two in game eleven, but both players remained rock solid under the pressure until they were locked at 7-7.

After a ferocious final set, in which Federer saved three break points, Nadal finally gained an advantage as Federer was forced into a forehand error. Nadal served out for the title and, despite more championship points saved by Federer, he took the match when Federer netted a forehand.

So...

...the rain, the delayed start, the breaks, the light, the uncertainty of whether the match would finish on that day or not. All instrumental in this phenomenal match. All uncontrollable!

The rain didn't make it easier but you have to expect the worst and he's the worst opponent on the best court.[2]

Roger Federer, Tennis Player

Your Performance Environment...

... is complex, multidimensional, and dynamic. It can be unpredictable and change rapidly without warning. Even now Wimbledon has a roof over Centre Court, which reduces stoppages, but 'the roof effect' still has an uncontrollable influence on the match. Professor Steve Haake from Sheffield Hallam University pointed out that since it takes ten minutes to close the roof, the grass will still get damp when it rains, and the ball will fluff up due to moisture on the grass.[3] The ball consequently becomes less aerodynamic and slower. The change in temperature also affects the flight of the ball. There is no escaping uncontrollability.

In your performance environment, you had better acknowledge and accept that there are aspects of your world that you cannot control. But also, and more importantly, there are aspects that you *can* control and this is the focus of chapter 6.

Scientific research and consultancy experience tells us that focusing on the aspects of performance(s) that we can control helps us to focus on the right things, whilst also facilitating a sense of belief that performance is achievable. Thinking and acting on factors that you can control helps to eliminate any focus on irrational, illogical, and unhelpful thoughts which are often optimized by a focus on uncontrollable aspects of our world. So being in control is a crucial resource in The MAPP, helping you to harness your self-confidence and direct your focus towards *what can be achieved*.

Too often in our applied work we find ourselves reminding athletes from a variety of domains to focus on the things they can control. This is often easier said than done, of course, but this chapter will help provide you with the tools you will need to make sure that you are always focusing on what you can control.

*Recognize that there are aspects of your world that
you cannot control. But more importantly, that
there are aspects that you can control.*

Rather than list the 'uncontrollables' for you, it makes more sense for
you to do this for yourself. After all, you are the athlete! So in the
table below identify what you can and cannot control during a
performance.

Uncontrollable	Controllable

Let's look critically at your list. In the left column should be aspects
that are largely external to you. That is, those aspects are controlled
by external factors that may be influenced by you, but ultimately are
uncontrollable. For example, many athletes place enormous value in
what their coaches and teammates think of them and are motivated
in part by the judgment of those significant people. This is
understandable because coaches and teammates can facilitate your
progression and achievement, and it is possible to influence what
those important people think of you by performing better and

achieving more in your sport. Ultimately, though, if they think you're useless then there might be little you can do to change opinions. You cannot control what they think. And it may come as a surprise, but you cannot control whether you get into the team, get selected for that championship, or get chosen to take that penalty. You see, these outcomes require the influence of various uncontrollable factors: your opponents, your coaches, your teammates, the 'ever-moving goal posts' of sport performance.

You have power over your mind – not outside events. Remember this and you will find strength.[4]

Marcus Aurelius, Roman Emperor (161-180AD)

In the right column of the table should be aspects that are in your direct control. Typically, these aspects are internal to you, but not always. For example, there are many inanimate objects that you can have direct control over. If I want to move the chair I am sitting on right now - writing this chapter - I can just stand up and move it (hopefully I remember to replace it before I sit back down). But the sport performance environment is rarely inanimate, so it makes more sense to focus on the aspects that are *internal* to you. At the same time it is important to recognize and crucially accept the uncontrollable aspects as part of the wonderful landscape of your performance environment.

The truth is, all stressful situations have an element of uncertainty, it's part of what makes those situations stressful. Think about attending trials for a place in a team. Whether you get a place in the team is hinged on the decisions of the head coach and the scouts. You may be confident in your ability to perform well and give a good account of yourself, but you don't know that you will (definitely) get a place because you cannot control the opinions of the head coach and the scouts. In fact, you may have experienced times when you have performed well but still have not been given the credit you "deserve" from others. Whilst this kind of situation undoubtedly leads to feelings of frustration, you cannot control what others think of you. However, focusing on aspects of your performance that you need to do to perform well, will bring a sense of control and on most occasions lead to better performance. It therefore makes sense to avoid wasting important mental energy and resources on things which you cannot control, but rather become selfish in choosing the things to think about prior to, during, and following performance.

Recognizing what you can control, and what you cannot control, has been known for centuries. To reiterate Marcus Aurelius, the second century Roman Emperor: "You have power over your mind - not outside events." Seems simple doesn't it? So how can we move forward with this effective 'Be in Control' thinking?

Focus on aspects of performance that you can control.

Go back to your list in the table and add to it (or remove stuff) based on what you have read so far in this chapter. Indeed, this will no doubt be an ever-changing and evolving list as you progress in your career, so keep it up-to-date and keep it fresh.

Hold on one second. You cannot control what others think of you? You cannot control how your competitors perform? And you cannot control decisions made by others such as selection? Surely this goes against what we said in the previous chapter? Uncertainty. Uncontrollability. Surely they will damage self-belief? This sounds a recipe for disaster doesn't it? No!

Facing uncertainty is no problem as long as you have the resources to cope with the performance demands. Look back to chapter 2 at The MAPP. As long as you are self-confident, are focused on what you can control, and what you can achieve - then you will flourish amidst uncertainty. Remember, there is no guaranteed success, there are simply too many uncontrollables, but by focusing on developing your personal resources you can ensure that you fulfil your potential, thus tipping the balance in your favour.

114

Focusing on aspects of performance you cannot control
wastes important mental resources and energy.

Control is In Hand

From research and work with elite athletes, key controllables for performance can be identified. Much of what we detail, in line with the rest of the book, is psychological in nature, but there are some important practical aspects that can inject control into the sport performance environment. We like to think of these five controllables as fingers on a hand that can be manipulated to exercise control over any performance situation.

Do not let circumstances control you.
You change your circumstances.[5]

Jackie Chan, Actor

115

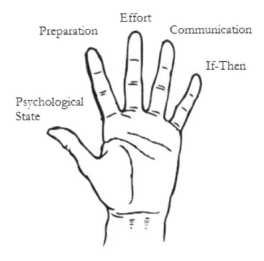

We will cover each of the 5 controllables in detail but here is a brief idea of what each controllable is about:

1. Psychological State: *Telling yourself the right things*

2. Preparation: *Being routined in the lead up to your performance*

3. Effort: *Going over and above in pursuit of excellence*

4. Communication: *Receiving and delivering the right messages*

5. If-Then: *Planning to achieve*

1. Psychological State

Let's face it, this book is about how to get into the most effective psychological state for sport performance, so you should be well on your way to this first step. However, as touched upon in chapter 5, work with professional athletes has shown how one strategy, in particular, is very effective in directing thoughts and behaviours: Self-Talk.

Self-Talk

Do or do not, there is no try.[6]

Yoda, Jedi Grand Master

Self-talk is simply about finding the right words to say to yourself at the right times. Self-talk can be used in lots of highly effective ways. Here we will first take you through the process of stopping unhelpful thoughts. Then you will learn to change unhelpful thoughts to helpful thoughts, and then develop effective self-statements or "cue phrases". These cue phrases trigger desired psychological states such as self-confidence, assertiveness, and composure.

My free-kick secret? I just look at the net and say 'Take the kick, Cristiano.'[7]

Cristiano Ronaldo, Footballer, FIFA player of the year 2013

In a hugely engaging article by Ferris Jabr in Scientific American Mind[8], self-talk (or inner speech) is recognized as "a ready source of motivation, confidence and guidance in all kinds of scenarios – giving a presentation, hitting the gym or asking someone on a date". So it comes as no surprise that self-talk is one of the most frequently and widely used skills among elite athletes because the concept is logical and highly effective. This is illustrated beautifully by Kellie Wells, who won a Bronze medal at the London 2012 Olympics in the 100m hurdles:

"If you think you can't, you won't, and if you think you can, you will. When I'm tired at practice, I tell myself that I'm not tired, and I can push through. If you tell yourself you're tired or if you tell yourself you're sick, your body is going to follow the mind."[9]

We will start by asking you some questions. How do you want to feel before you perform? Take a specific situation (e.g., competition, trial, free throw) from the past and think about how you felt before your best performance. Would you want to feel like that again? Or maybe think of a specific situation from the past in which you did not do so well. Perhaps if you had felt differently you would have performed better. What would you change? Most athletes we work with report wanting to feel three things: confident, composed, and ready. They usually want to feel this way right before they perform. Waiting for the referee's whistle for the match to begin, stretching in the holding area, waiting to be called for your sprint, sitting on the grid just before the lights go out at the Grand Prix. Maybe this is how you want to feel too?

Self-talk can be used to combat unhelpful and unwanted thoughts.

So how can you get there? How can you make sure you are confident, composed, and ready in the moments before you perform? The first step is recognizing and dealing with the thoughts that are trying to prevent you from getting into this winning mindset. Let's start by recognizing the unhelpful thoughts. To do this, ideally you would record your thoughts in a diary prior to a competition a few times and look critically at what you are saying to yourself. By all means do this. But for now, picture yourself in the final moments prior to three highly important situations you will face at some point in the near future in your sport, or have faced in the past. Write these situations in the boxes at the top of the table overleaf. Next, write down the negative thoughts you may have, have had, or are having, about the situations.

Situation 1:	Situation 2:	Situation 3:
Negative Thoughts:	Negative Thoughts:	Negative Thoughts:

There is good evidence that merely trying to stop yourself from having negative thoughts will actually increase the likelihood and intensity of unwanted thoughts.[10] For example, try not to think of a pink elephant. Don't think about the pink elephant whatever you do.

Thinking of the pink elephant? That's no surprise. By suppressing negative thoughts you only bring attention to those thoughts at times when you should be focusing on positive thoughts (more on thought suppression in chapter 7). So now you have recognized the negative thoughts in the boxes above, you can move onto strategies to help yourself think positively. After all, positive thinking is aligned with many psychological benefits including increased concentration, confidence, motivation, and control.

Empty Your Head

One effective strategy is called "empty your head" and can be done the night before (or the morning of) your sport performance. Instead of trying to stop the negative thoughts by desperately telling yourself not to think in that way, it is better to allow yourself to have those thoughts at specific times in the lead-up to your performance. Expressing your thoughts instead of suppressing them means that you are no longer wasting time and mental energy trying to battle your negative thoughts. But importantly, you have set aside a specific time in which to think in this way - a safe distance from your performance. For example, you may decide that the day before your competition at 12pm you will sit down and write about your negative thoughts in all their glorious details. After you have done this, read what you have described and marvel at the creative ways in which you have pictured your demise.

That's my gift. I let that negativity roll off me like water off a duck's back... If you can overcome that, fights are easy.[11]

George Foreman, Boxer

This may seem odd. It is known as a *paradoxical strategy*, and the trick is not to suppress negative thoughts, but to let them flow into your head and play out unrestricted. Think about the very thing you don't want to happen. Missing that penalty, timing your race incorrectly, making double faults, missing putts. Spend a moment doing this. If you do this properly you will probably start to realize that, similar to the Smart Thinking idea, actually these thoughts will not kill you and that they are a normal part of competing.

Emptying your head involves expressing all of the negative thoughts you have prior to, and even after, competition.

The thoughts you will have had when placed in competitive situations will mirror those of other athletes. It is very common to think negatively. By first being aware of your thoughts, then recognizing that they are typical of such situations you can now begin to neutralize them to maximize and unlock your potential. In addition, by allowing yourself to think negatively (that is, by exposing yourself to undesired outcomes and thoughts of failure and embarrassment) you may actually fear the outcome much less. This is known as *desensitization* and it simply means that because you are making yourself think about the thing you fear; you *learn* not to fear it (alongside other strategies which we will cover in chapter 9). By accepting that failure happens and by allowing yourself to think negatively in a controlled manner, you remove the need for thought suppression.

Triggers

Eliminate all negative thoughts until they don't exist.[12]

Marvin Hagler, Boxer

So let's get back to the moments before the big performance. You have recognized your negative thoughts and have let yourself dwell already. So there is no need for those thoughts here and now. Now is the time for positive and helpful thinking. When you are in the moments before performance you need only think about what you will do to perform well. Be careful, this is not about wishful thinking. Think of this as filling your head with helpful thoughts so that the negative thoughts can't get in.

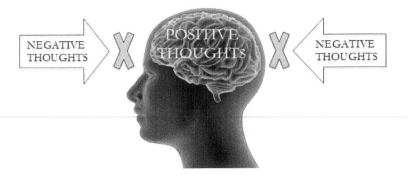

These positive thoughts can be triggered by key phrases that you have decisively allocated to the thoughts and feelings that will help you perform.

Choose the positive. You have choice, you are master of your attitude, choose the positive, the constructive. Optimism is a faith that leads to success.[13]

Bruce Lee, Actor

The idea of using trigger words or phrases is very popular with elite athletes and can be highly motivational. Specifically here, we are talking about allocating words to specific thoughts so that with a quick reminder, you can access the thought and let your mind drift into positivity. Put crudely, tell your brain what you want it to think and feel. The quote that starts this section gives a nice example of this. Cristiano Ronaldo is telling his brain what to do: "take the kick" – it's a very instructional self-talk. The first step is to figure out what your positive thoughts will be. Luckily, you have been through the visualization ammunition elements of chapter 5 so you have plenty of positive experiences to draw from to inspire these positive thoughts. In the left column of the table below, write down the positive thoughts you want to have prior to your performance following the example on the first row.

Positive thought	Triggers
I know that when I'm fully prepared I can perform well in any situation. I remember in the past, I have performed well when I have felt prepared.	I'm ready!

Now you have allocated some triggers to your positive thoughts, the next step is to practice this strategy. Remember, just like physical and technical skills, mental skills take practice to learn and master. Reaffirm these triggers as often as you can. Use the trigger and let your head flood with the positive thoughts you have identified as helping you to fulfil your potential. We often find that athletes we work with want to create cue cards (usually the size of a business card) or signs displaying their triggers. Put these in your kit bag or on your screen saver and really work towards creating a positive culture for yourself.

My thoughts before a big race are usually pretty simple. I tell myself: Get out of the blocks, run your race, stay relaxed. If you run your race, you'll win... channel your energy. Focus.[14]

Carl Lewis, Track and Field Athlete

2. Preparation

Give me six hours to chop down a tree, and I will spend the first four hours sharpening the axe.[15]

Abraham Lincoln, 16th President of the United States of America

Picture the scene. It is 10pm and Alice has read over the golf course details for the last time. Her journey is planned out, and her kit is ironed and hanging up on the bedroom door ready for tomorrow. It's cereal, toast, and fruit juice for breakfast. She sets her alarm for 6:55am. She allows herself to think once more about what she needs to do to perform well tomorrow, and then reaffirms that she has done everything she can to ensure she fulfils her potential. After emptying her head she drifts off to sleep in a calm and confident haze.

On waking, her morning is planned. Shower at 7am, ready in the kit she has prepared at 7:45am, breakfast at 8am, out the door and in her car at 8:30am. She knows the route to the course and has given herself 90 minutes to make a 60-minute journey. On arrival she knows where to park and where to register for the tournament as she has checked beforehand. After registering, she enters the warm-up area and practices her swing while she waits for her performance to begin.

She visualizes her opening drive off the first tee, the approach, the swing, the feelings of confidence and control she will express on connecting with the ball for the first time. She reminds herself of how "strong, confident, and composed" she is. As she approaches the tee for the first time she feels her heart pounding and reminds herself: "I am ready". For today is the most important day of her professional career. Today she will compete in her first pro golf tournament.

"I am building a fire, and every day I train, I add more fuel. At just the right moment, I light the match."[16]

Mia Hamm, Soccer Player

Above, Alice has engaged in many preparatory strategies to ensure she is ready to perform when the time comes. Her behaviours are constructive (having her kit ready) and her thoughts are self-promotional ("I am ready"). But most importantly, because she has engaged in these thoughts and behaviours she knows that she has done everything in her power to ensure she fulfils her potential at the tournament.

Preparation is certainly about the weeks and months of hard work that lead up to that all-important performance. But all that is in vain if you are not able to fulfil that potential on the day. Here, we talk about how to make sure - on the day leading up to your performance - you are 100% ready to perform.

The real essence of what we are saying throughout this book is that whatever your performance, whatever your sport or role within your sport, be excellent or be elite in whatever you do – including your thoughts, behaviours, preparation, and recovery. Being excellent in these areas means that you will tip the balance in your favour and fulfil your potential.

Largely, being excellent is about developing and engaging in a pre-performance routine that brings consistency and controllability to your preparation. In addition, and as discussed in chapter 5, preparation is a key source of self-confidence, magnifying the importance of preparing fully. So next, we will help you to develop your own pre-performance routine.

Your Pre-Performance Routine

You will often see elite athletes going through a consistent routine prior to their performance. For example, consider Olympic swimmers. Most, if not all, enter the swimming arena wearing headphones and are most likely listening to a favourite or motivational track to help them get into the right mental and physical state for the upcoming event. Furthermore, next time you watch professional golfers on the TV you will observe the consistency with which they approach each shot. Often they will take a look at the target, have a few practice swings, address the ball, check their balance, and then initiate their actual swing (no doubt accompanied by a swing thought).

A great example of an elite athlete with a pre-performance routine is Mo Farah. In his autobiography "Twin Ambitions" he gives a great insight into what he did prior to his 10,000m gold medal-winning performance at the 2012 Olympics.[17]

"Every athlete has a routine they like to stick to. I like to shave my head. Then I'll listen to some tunes. Depending on my mood, it'll be some Tupac or maybe Dizzee Rascal. If I want something a bit more chilled, I'll put on some Somali music.

After lunch I grab a couple of hours' sleep. Then I wait.

Three hours before the start of the race, I head down to the stadium and make my way to the warm-up area.

Twenty minutes before a race, I'll normally drink some coffee to wake me up... I take a second espresso... I feel this massive caffeine high come on. I'm buzzing.

At that moment, I am more pumped than ever before in my life.

Everything has been leading to this. I'm looking around and telling myself, "This is my moment. This is it. I am ready to race."

Having a consistent routine prior to an important event or situation offers many benefits. Routines foster confidence, develop a focus on relevant behaviours and thoughts, and bring an element of control to unpredictable situations. After all, it is you and only you who can control the thoughts and behaviours that precede your performance. The main advantage of having a routine is that if you are focusing on your routine, then you are unlikely to become distracted by external uncontrollable factors that you know are there, but which you do not need to focus on right now.

Top athletes perform well and feel confident when they have prepared thoroughly. One of the main predictors of Olympic athletes' confidence levels prior to an Olympic event is the extent to which they have prepared. Thus, if their training has been appropriate and they feel like they have left no stone unturned then ultimately they feel efficacious in their ability to deliver the goods at the appropriate time. Therefore it makes perfect sense to not only prepare well but to think strategically about what you need to do in your preparation to allow you to maximize your potential. To help you do this we will now consider how to devise a pre-performance routine.

Routines bring consistency to performance preparation. With consistency comes confidence.

Developing a routine can be considered within the wider issue of preparing well. Therefore, successful athletes generally look after themselves by eating the right things, making sure they are hydrated, training smart, taking time to recover, reflecting effectively, and building self-confidence by tapping into their main sources of confidence as indicated in chapter 5.

As highlighted above, in the build-up to competitions, you can be more strategic in your preparation to bring you more control. The example below demonstrates how a soccer athlete may prepare prior to a match. As you can see, the first important step is to identify the *key time points* at which you will engage in performance preparation thoughts and behaviours. With many athletes we have worked with, this is typically:

1. The night before competition

2. The morning of competition

3. The journey to competition

4. Arrival at the venue

5. Changing rooms

6. Immediately prior to competition

At each point above the athlete engages in very specific and consistent thoughts and behaviours that will contribute to their performance. For example, the night before a competition the athlete may allow himself/herself to worry about the performance by using the "empty your head" exercise, as well as getting their kit ready for departure to the venue in the morning. Immediately prior to competition the athlete may be running through their mind only the aspects they know they need to do well to perform to their potential. This may include visualizing the perfect execution of their first pass/tackle/shot at goal (in soccer/football for example).

The point is, at each time point there is a *reason* for engaging in that thinking and that behaviour, so the routine is meaningful and can have an impact on performance. Below, we have identified the key time points for preparing for competition. We would advise that after reading this book, you complete the table on the next page as fully as possible in relation to upcoming and frequent important performances you are approaching, including all the knowledge you have gleaned about the psychology of optimal performance so far.

But for now, identify some of the thoughts and behaviours that you feel will help you prepare for your next competition in the table so you can add to it later.

Time Point	Helpful Thoughts	Helpful Behaviours
Night Before		
Morning Of		
Journey		
Arrival		
Changing Rooms		
Directly Prior		

The key to making sure your routines work well is to practice them prior to a less important event or in training situations. This process allows for refinement and reflection on the content to enable you to develop a routine, which really does aid your sport performance. We often find that getting athletes to think about what they need to do to perform well by developing a routine reinforces how they can become more efficient with their thinking. That is, they can follow a set routine so that their thoughts are not all over the place prior to performance. Importantly, routines help athletes to maintain an element of control when facing challenging events in which distractions are usually lurking.

It is important to also note that having a pre-performance routine is *not the same* as being superstitious. One professional golfer we worked with believed that an extreme pre-performance routine, comprising of a series of superstitions, provided him with divine influence and the luck to control the weather, so that it was not windy. Very quickly we helped him realize that this extreme focus on external, uncontrollable events was a waste of mental energy and detrimental to his mindset and performance. The interesting thing is that - prior to working with him - he had thought that his approach was the only way to think on the golf course and maximize his potential. Having a consistent routine is about *controlling the controllables*, not trying to control the uncontrollables.

Flying by the seat of your pants precedes crashing by the seat of your pants.[18]

Bill Walsh, NFL Coach of the Year 1981 and 1984

3. Effort

A lifetime of training for just ten seconds.

Jesse Owens, Track Athlete

Effort is a choice and you are the controller of when, and how, to apply this effort. You decide how much time and energy you devote to all aspects of your life. The idea that some people are born special and have a natural ability to succeed in sport is grinding to a halt as we recognize that the real secret to athletic success is effort, persistence, and commitment.

In Matthew Syed's highly influential book "Bounce", he talks about the myth of talent, and the idea that it is hard work that leads to success, not natural ability. Even those who seem to have a 'natural gift', have to work hard to succeed. There is a really nice extract from the book to illustrate the point...

"Examine any sporting life where success has arrived early and the same story just keeps repeating itself. David Beckham, for example, would take a football to the local park in east London as a young child and kick it from precisely the same spot for hour upon hour. 'His dedication was breathtaking,' his father has said. 'It sometimes seemed that he lived on the local field.' Beckham concurs. 'My secret is practice,' he said. 'I have always believed that if you want to achieve anything special in life you have to work, work, and then work some more.'"[19]

Effort is a choice.
You either choose to work hard or not.

Chapter 6

So we know that top athletes often work harder and smarter, keep going when things are tough, and are resilient in the face of setbacks. There are numerous illustrations of elite athletes turning up for training early and staying late to learn and perfect skills whilst making a commitment to 'living' the life of a professional. Plainly, by realizing that your skills and abilities are adaptable, shapeable, and transferable, you will realize that you can have control over your success like never before.

The notion that it is those who dedicate themselves to succeeding who eventually prevail is not new. Aristotle, the Greek philosopher (384-322 BC) who wrote on subjects such as physics, metaphysics, poetry, theatre, music, logic, rhetoric, linguistics, politics, government, ethics, biology, and zoology (a busy man!) said that: "Excellence is an art won by training and habituation. We do not act rightly because we have virtue or excellence, but we rather have those because we have acted rightly. We are what we repeatedly do. Excellence, then, is not an act but a habit."[20]

We are what we repeatedly do. So success, or excellence, comes from hard work, not luck, chance, or genetics. In fact, the golf champion Gary Player famously said that, "The harder I practice the luckier I get."[21]

Simply put, success is born from effort and persistence, and therefore, knowing where to direct your effort is crucial. Let's look at a case-study, the 2013 FIFA World Player of the Year, and one of the greatest soccer athletes of all time: Cristiano Ronaldo.

"I am not a perfectionist, but I like to feel that things are done well. More important than that, I feel an endless need to learn, to improve, to evolve, not only to please the coach and the fans, but also to feel satisfied with myself. It is my conviction that there are no limits to learning, and that it can never stop, no matter what our age."[22]

Ronaldo wasn't born gifted - nobody is, remember. But his early years helped him to develop his soccer abilities, a time when all he wanted to do was play soccer. His godfather said, "He loved the game so much he'd miss meals or escape out of his bedroom window with a ball when he was supposed to be doing his homework."[23] Like any child who enjoys soccer, he lived and breathed the game. But these developmental experiences are common for many athletes who do not make it to the top of their field. The most significant thing about Ronaldo, and lots of other highly decorated athletes, is that he *continues* to live and breathe the game.

Mike Clegg, ex-Manchester United power development coach, gave a fascinating account of Ronaldo's training ethic in the Manchester Evening News.[24] Clegg explained: "He took on a new level of total dedication to his training because he wanted to be the best footballer in the world. I've seen players train themselves into the ground because of insufficient knowledge, but Ronaldo was more intelligent than that. He'd train hard, but he'd listen to the specialists around him, the coaches, the manager, the other players. He took their advice in pursuit of personal excellence."

So Ronaldo didn't just push himself physically, he thought smartly about where to direct his effort. It's not good enough to expend maximal effort in doing the same things over and over again, day to day. It's about recognizing where your effort can have the most impact for your progression towards what you want to *become*, not what you are now.

Clegg continued: "Ronaldo would also arrive early so he could prepare properly. He'd be in the gym with me doing core work, then he'd do activation, then his actual football training."

Ronaldo didn't just go through the motions. He made sure that his time at the club was maximized by using the time before training to specifically develop one of the important physical aspects of his game: his strength. If you are a 100m sprinter where the vital part of your performance is getting out of the blocks as quickly as possible, it makes sense that you would allocate time to develop your reactions to the gun, not just the explosive power you have in your arms and legs. But how much do you really focus on developing these 'softer skills'?

Also, Clegg explained that things didn't stop when the formal training was over. "Training done, that was the point at which most footballers went home. Cristiano would come back into the gym and do some power work for his legs. Then he would go home, eat the right food, swim, sleep, where I'm sure he dreamed about football, and come back in the next morning. He did that for five or six years and, knitted together, that made him become the player who was sold for £80m."

Look at any top athlete. Their working day does not start when they arrive at training and finish when they leave. Those might be their official training hours, but to really fulfil their potential, it's the extra time they put in after their structured training time that is crucial.

We are not saying that training all hours is the answer; but working smartly towards what you want to become requires extra effort that can eat into your 'personal time'. This might include additional training of mental and tactical skills to fill in any gaps in sport knowledge, staying fit and healthy using cutting edge nutrition, and of course reading this book! Effort is not simply about how hard you try when performing, it is more about the persistence and dedication you have, and how you can direct your energy to the right things.

Doctors and scientists said that breaking the four-minute mile was impossible, that one would die in the attempt. Thus, when I got up from the track after collapsing at the finish line, I figured I was dead.[25]

Roger Bannister, after becoming the first person to break the four-minute mile in 1952

Complete the table below. It will help you to understand where you can direct your effort to help fulfil your potential. Importantly, everything in this table should be *controllable by you*.

What I need to do to get to the next level	What I am going to do to make it happen
[example] Develop more attuned concentration	a. Take that sport psychology course I've been meaning to take for a while. b. Reflect on my concentration levels each week and identify areas of strength and possible improvements. c. Ask my coaches and teammates to complete anonymous feedback forms each month on my concentration.

Recognizing the areas in which your effort should be invested is central to achieving all that you want to achieve. By maintaining your self-confidence (see chapter 5), preparing well, and directing your effort smartly, you are leaving very little to chance. You are taking control of your performance and career success.

"Everyone predicted that Sonny Liston would destroy me. And he was scary. But it's a lack of faith that makes people afraid of meeting challenges, and I believed in myself. I was confident I could whup him. So what I did was, I studied his style, I trained hard, and I watched Liston outside the ring. I went to his training camp and tried to understand what went on inside his head, so later on I could mess with his mind. And all the time, I was talking, talking. That way, I figured Liston would get so mad that, when the fight came, he'd try to kill me and forget everything he knew about boxing."[26] - Muhammad Ali

4. Communication

As you will no doubt be aware you communicate all of the time (whether through verbal or non-verbal means). However, you may not necessarily be aware of how your communication is interpreted and received by those you come into contact with. Understanding the nature and impact of your verbal and non-verbal communication on others is hugely important.

However, arguably more important is *taking control of your communication* to maximize your emotions and the emotions of those around you. For example, the verbal and non-verbal communication you present prior to a stressful or pressured event will have a large effect on the thoughts, feelings, and behaviours of those listening. On too many occasions we have seen coaches deliver what they consider to be inspirational speeches prior to important sporting events only to hear them use ironic statements such as 'don't mess up' and 'don't make mistakes'. Consequently, they have inadvertently provided ironic messages that potentially reinforce negative thoughts and create intense stress for performers.

Delivering the Right Messages

Sir Alex Ferguson, when he was manager of Manchester United, was a master of taking control of his communication prior to important matches to maximize the confidence of his players. For example, in his press conferences, he would often report that he 'trusted' his players, wanted them to 'express' themselves and 'enjoy' the challenge of the game, whilst being 'excited' about the potential of the team.

We also know that emotions are contagious and that if we demonstrate stress through body language and mannerisms then those around us pick up on this. For example, consider a dentist's waiting room. Before your arrival you may feel relaxed and not particularly concerned about going to see your dentist. However, when sitting in the waiting room you notice a person opposite you biting their nails, and fidgeting repeatedly in their chair. Instantly, you make the assumption that they are nervous and apprehensive. Very quickly you start to model their behaviour and begin to experience some of the concerns that they are clearly feeling. This example illustrates that you have a responsibility to yourself but also to those around you to ensure that your verbal and non-verbal communication is controlled in a manner to maximize sport performance. Accordingly, it is important that verbal instructions you provide to individuals prior to competing remind them of success, their strengths, and aspects of the role or performance they can control. Do not provide information which completely stresses them out.

Emotions are contagious. Therefore, you should work hard to manage the emotions you convey to others.

One way to assist taking control of your communication is to get someone to record you before an important performance and then reflect on how you behaved and communicated. For example, get a recording of you walking out onto the field, court, or track. You will very quickly realize whether you are being effective. From here, choose a role-model who you think demonstrates the types of communication you wish to present and begin to draw inspiration from them alongside asking yourself the key question: 'how would [role-model] behave in this situation?'.

One athlete we worked with observed that his body language during events gave off the wrong impression. In essence, he remarked (when we showed him film footage) that he looked beaten and nervous before he started. After some reflection he observed that Cristiano Ronaldo often smiles when under pressure on the football pitch. The athlete further commented that he rarely saw this in sport. We worked with him to recognize the influence of smiling under pressure not only for himself but for his teammates and opposition. As a result he felt more composed and in control, and actually enjoyed performing more. This is crucial for any performance.

Receiving the Right Messages

Another aspect of communication is taking control of how you receive information from others such as coaches and teammates. For example, consider how you typically react to stressful or disappointing news? Think about the messages that you are conveying through your reactions. Are they helpful or detrimental to those around you and yourself?

One aspect we work on with athletes is their reactions to success and failure. The crux is that you can control how you react to information you receive from others to maintain emotional control and to have a positive effect on those around you.

Consider a situation where you receive criticism from your coach or manager - how would you feel? Is your body language negative? Do you lose control of your verbal and non-verbal communication? Do you say something that you will regret later on? Does your body language look defeatist?

If you answered 'yes' to any of the questions then consider how you could take better control and modify your reactions. An effective strategy we use with athletes is to break their reactions down into five component parts:

The 5Rs of Communication

Receive – Don't deflect or remonstrate at this stage. Take on-board the coach's views and opinions ready for logical processing.

Reflect – Take some time. Even if it is seconds. Consider the information and the context in which it was delivered to you.

Regroup – Having collected your thoughts, prepare for your response. In other words, move past the receiving stage and towards the delivery stage and prepare for your reaction to the information.

React – Take care to control and modify your behavioural reactions here. Rarely does losing your temper serve you well. Try to remain composed and remind yourself that people cannot 'make' you feel angry, or upset (see Think Smart in chapter 3)

Respond – Perhaps the situation calls for a verbal response, or requires you to act out a task. Remember that you are in control of this response and that whatever you say or do is an extension of yourself. Having completed the preceding Rs, your response should be calculated and directed at producing the best results for you and your company.

A useful approach is to ask (once again): 'What would my role model do? In turn, try replaying some critical scenarios in your head and see yourself taking better control by using the 5Rs. Repeat this process until you control how you deal with the situation. How did it feel? What did you look like? We hope that, with practice, you should be able to experience better control and coping. Indeed, such awareness of communication control can be transmitted to those around you - your teammates, friends, partners, and coaches. Very quickly you can begin to help individuals to provide more effective and controlled verbal and non-verbal communication.

In the previous chapter we talked about 'embodied cognition' and the idea that the way you think and feel can be determined by the way you act. Research has found that adopting positive body language when receiving feedback leads to greater feelings of pride about performance. So regardless of the message, *act positively on receipt*.

5. If-Then

The fifth controllable in this chapter owes much to the work of Dr. Peter M. Gollwitzer, Professor of Psychology at New York University. Gollwitzer put forward the idea of implementation intentions[27], which are more commonly known as "if-then plans".

If-then plans help us to formulate how to achieve a desired goal in a specific and controllable way. The "if" part reflects an opportunity or an obstacle. The "then" part reflects goal-directed behaviour in response to the "if" part. For example, on approaching an important competition you might say, "IF I feel nervous before the event, THEN I will remind myself that I am a prepared and capable athlete." Or "IF my coach asks me to demonstrate something that I am not skilled in, THEN I will admit the fact and remain composed".

You can even make these if-then plans more broad. For example, you could say "IF I want to get that dream contract, THEN every day I will work towards being a better athlete." Or "IF I want to be successful in this sport, THEN I will develop the skills I need to fulfil my potential."

Having if-then plans is far better than simply stating that you *want* something. Merely saying "I want to get that dream contract" is rational and may be accurate, but does very little in the way of directing your actions towards getting that dream contract. By using if-then plans you are able to not only recognize that desire or goal, but you are also able to direct your behaviour towards making that desire become a reality.

These if-then plans have been linked to enhanced goal achievement, helping people to take control of their actions towards their targets, and in response to setbacks. A rugby athlete we worked with was really struggling with his training regime as a large portion of it was self-directed in the athlete's own time. Suffice it to say, he was struggling to get motivated when he was in charge of his training. In the mornings he would wake up and press the snooze button on his alarm until it was too late to go for a run. He procrastinated about getting up to train right up until he reached the point where it became logistically impossible to fit training into his morning. So we implemented if-then plans with him. Here are some of them:

- IF I wake up and I'm not in the mood for training, THEN I will remind myself of what I want to achieve this year

- IF I need to train in the morning, THEN I will make sure my kit is packed the night before

- IF I want to be the best I can possibly be, THEN I will stay committed to my training night and day

As you will notice in his plans, all of the aspects are controllable by him. This is very important because if the "then" part of any plan is not controllable, then there is no guarantee that you can make it happen. The rugby athlete above was able to maintain his training regime and now prides himself on his commitment and determination through physical hardship.

Your If-Then Plans

Setting up if-then plans is quite easy, but they can have a huge impact on your sport performance. Simply put, you are completing the x and y in the following equation: if x happens, then I will y.

We will help you to develop some if-then strategies via a structured step-by-step process. By following the steps, you will be able to implement these plans in your day-to-day training and crucially when approaching important performance situations.

Step 1. Have a clear goal.

Make sure that your goal is not ambiguous (e.g., lacking clarity or definiteness). A good example would be the goal of getting that contract, or mastering a skill, or working hard each day in training. In the box below, write down your top five goals for this year. We have completed an example to show you. Remember, be specific.

My Goals
1.
2.
3.
4.
5.
Example: Get my contract renewed for another 5 years

Step 2. Identify the potential obstacles.

All goals have obstacles. But the important thing here is to identify the significant obstacles that you need to plan for. For example, your goal of becoming the top goal scorer in your team may be hindered by an injury. Or your goal of hitting your PB at the next race might be hindered by a sudden downpour of rain before the event. Below, write down the significant obstacles you may face to achieving the goals you wrote down in step 1.

Potential Obstacles
1.
2.
3.
4.
5.
Example: An injury that puts me out for 3 months

Step 3. The IF.

Now you can start to develop your if-then plans to help overcome the obstacles to your goals by first framing your "If" statements. The "if" parts can include the obstacle or the goal. For example, you could say "IF I am to get that dream contract..." or "IF I get injured for 3 months..." Have a go below.

IF parts
1.
2.
3.
4.
5.
Example: IF I get an injury for 3 months...

Step 4. The "THEN".

This part is obviously really important as it is the response to your "if" statement. Essentially you are making a plan so that if the identified obstacle occurs, then you will know what to do and how to do it. This is where the control takes place.

You can be in charge of how you react to setbacks and can be in charge of how you strive for your goals.

The "then" part can involve thinking, doing, or even ignoring something. That is, you could have a number of controllable reactions to the same event. For example, one athlete we worked with was making the step up from academy level to Pro level. One day after normal academy training he was asked to take part in training with the Pro team. This took him by surprise but he had thought about what he would do beforehand, and as a consequence had various strategies in place: (a) keep calm and prepare as normal

(b) remind self of good skill and ability (c) behave professionally and be positive on the field. The if-then plan went like this: IF I am asked to train with the Pros, THEN I will keep calm, remind myself that I am a skilled and highly trained athlete, and be professional and positive. So although nervous inside, the plan helped him to perform well in this difficult and unpredictable situation. Your turn below.

THEN parts
1.
2.
3.
4.
5.
Example: THEN I will commit fully to rehabilitation and take on the advice of experts

As with all of the chapters in this book, practice and reinforce your if-then plans to make them stick. Refresh your memory of them especially before important situations where your best performance is necessary. And crucially, add to them, change them, keep them fresh and up-to-date.

Why it Works

There are many reasons as to why if-then plans can help you to reach your goals. First, and in line with this chapter, they allow you to control your reactions to setbacks. By having plans in place you will not be caught off-guard and have to respond in ways that do not show you in your best light.

Second, they help to narrow your options in any given situation. Decision making is a lot easier when you only have one choice! Imagine not having a plan should you unexpectedly qualify for an Olympic final. Your head would be spinning trying to figure out what you need to do to prepare for the biggest event of your career. But by adopting "IF I qualify for the final, THEN I will remain calm and approach the event in the same way as I would any other event" you have a strategy in place to make sure you don't come off the rails.

Third, because you have a plan in place, in the event of adverse occurrences, you don't need to waste time and energy on devising an appropriate plan in the moment. In other words, you have an automatic response to the setback that you won't forget or need to devise at a moment's notice.

Last, but certainly not least, by having if-then plans you are adding to your self-confidence as you are adding an extra fail-safe to your performance preparation. That is, you know you are prepared for whatever happens and therefore can be confident in your ability to react to setbacks in a positive and adaptive manner.

If-then plans allow you to control your reactions
to setbacks, speed up your decision making, and
can save time and energy.

Brief Summary

As you can see, there are many ways that you can focus on the controllable aspects of your performance environment.

It is important to recognize and accept uncontrollable aspects, but in the heat of sport performance, focusing on what you can control is vital. It is also important to realize that confidence and control are linked. In The MAPP, all of the resources are interconnected so that one influences another. If you are confident in your ability to perform when it really counts, and you feel you have control over the aspects of your performance that will allow you to succeed, then there is nothing between you and your goals.

How you frame those goals is also crucial. In chapter 7 you will learn how to ensure that you are always focused on what you want to achieve when you compete.

Most Important Point

Recognize the uncontrollable aspects of your performance, but only focus on what you can control in the lead up to your performance.

---

[1] Albert Ellis Tribute Book Series Launched (2006). *REBT Network*. Retrieved May 21, 2014, from http://www.rebtnetwork.org/library/Tribute_Book_Series.html

[2] Newbury, P. (2008, July 6). Rafael Nadal held off an incredible fightback from Roger Federer to win his first Wimbledon title and end the Swiss star's reign at the All England Club. *BBC*. Retrieved May 21, 2014, from http://news.bbc.co.uk/sport1/hi/tennis/7490443.stm

[3] McDermott, N (2011, June 23). How Centre Court's new roof puts a dampener on Andy Murray's serve. *Mail Online*. Retrieved May 21, 2014, from http://www.dailymail.co.uk/sciencetech/article-2007113/WIMBLEDON-2011-Centre-Courts-new-roof-puts-dampener-Andy-Murrays-serve.html

[4] Aurelius, M (2006). *Meditations*. London: Penguin Classics.

[5] Timeline photos (n. d.). *In Facebook.com*. Retrieved May 21, 2014, from https://www.facebook.com/jackie/photos/a.98876792317.90092.30382852317/10151913993652318/?type=1

[6] Quotes for Yoda (n. d.). *In IMDb*. Retrieved May 21, 2014, from http://www.imdb.com/character/ch0000015/quotes

[7] Cristiano Ronaldo best soccer quotes (n. d.). *In Ronaldo7.net*. Retrieved May 21, 2014, from http://www.ronaldo7.net/extra/quotes/cristiano-ronaldo-quotes.html

[8] Jabr, F. (2014). *Getting to know the voices in your head*. Scientific American Mind, 25, 1, 45-51.

[9] Matt. (2012, July 31). Top 25 Inspirational Quotes by Olympic Athletes. *In Share it Fitness*. Retrieved May 21, 2014, from http://blog.shareitfitness.com/2012/inspirational-quotes/

[10] Wegner, D. M., Ansfield, M. E., & Pilloff, D. (1998). The putt and the pendulum: Ironic effects of the mental control of action. *Psychological Science, 9*, 196-199.

[11] Carmichael, E. (n. d.). *From boxing to business: how foreman won the final rounds*. Retrieved May 21, 2014, from http://www.evancarmichael.com/Famous-Entrepreneurs/4589/From-Boxing-to-Business-How-Foreman-Won-the-Final-Rounds.html

[12] Gallagher, B (2003, November 7). *Hagler firmly in the Irish corner*. The Telegraph. Retrieved May 21, 2014, from http://www.telegraph.co.uk/sport/rugbyunion/international/ireland/2424869/Hagler-firmly-in-the-Irish-corner.html

[13] Little, J. (2000). *Striking thoughts: Bruce Lee's wisdom for daily living*. North Clarendon, Vermont: Tuttle Publishing

[14] Famous Sports Quotes. (n. d.). *In desktop-quotes.com*. Retrieved May 21, 2014, from http://www.desktop-quotes.com/famous-sports-quotes.html

[15] Pinola, M. (2011, June 21). Work Smarter and More Easily by "Sharpening Your Axe". *Lifehacker*. Retrieved May 21, 2014, from http://lifehacker.com/5814019/work-smarter-and-more-easily-by-sharpening-your-axe

[16] Matt. (2012, July 31). Top 25 inspirational quotes by Olympic athletes. *In shareitfitness.com*. Retrieved May 21, 2014, from http://blog.shareitfitness.com/2012/inspirational-quotes/

[17] Farah, M (2013). *Twin ambitions: My autobiography*. London: Hodder & Stoughton.

[18] Scott, A. (2013, June 21). From NESJ: Volunteer Coach: Create a plan to reach your goals. *NE Soccer Journal*. Retrieved May 21, 2014, from http://nesoccerjournal.com/news/players/coachs_corner/06-21-from-nesj-volunteer-coach-create-a-plan-to-reach-your-goals

[19] Syed, M. (2010). *Bounce*. London: Harper Collins Publishers.

[20] Aristotle quotes. (n.d.). *In thinkexist.com*. Retrieved May 21, 2014, from http://thinkexist.com/quotation/excellence_is_an_art_won_by_training_and/10320.html

[21] The harder I practice, the luckier I get (2010, July 14*). In quoteinvestigator.com*. Retrieved May 21, 2014, from http://quoteinvestigator.com/2010/07/14/luck/

[22] Cristiano Ronaldo best soccer quotes (n. d.). *In Ronaldo7.net*. Retrieved May 21, 2014, from http://www.ronaldo7.net/extra/quotes/cristiano-ronaldo-quotes.html

[23] Cristiano biography (n. d.). *In biography.com*. Retrieved May 21, 2014, from http://www.biography.com/people/cristiano-ronaldo-555730#awesm=~oErdy8anzjHzID

[24] Mitten, A (2013, March, 5). Ex-Reds' coach Mike Clegg on how Cristiano Ronaldo's total dedication to football was also in a league of its own. *Manchester Evening News*. Retrieved May 21, 2014, from http://www.manchestereveningnews.co.uk/sport/football/football-news/ex-reds-coach-mike-clegg-how-1719690

[25] Famous Sports Quotes. (n. d.). *In desktop-quotes.com*. Retrieved May 21, 2014, from http://www.desktop-quotes.com/famous-sports-quotes.html

[26] Micklos, J (2010). *Muhammad Ali: "I Am the Greatest"*. Berkeley Heights, NJ: Enslow Publishers.

[27] Gollwitzer, P. M., Wieber, F., Meyers, A. L., & McCrea, S. M. (2010). How to maximize implementation intention effects. In C. R. Agnew, D. E. Carlston, W. G. Graziano, J. R. Kelly (Eds.), *Then a miracle occurs: Focusing on behavior in social psychological theory and research* (pp.137-161). New York: Oxford Press.

Chapter 7: Focus On Success

Never let the fear of striking out get in your way.[1]

Babe Ruth, Baseball Player

There is a big difference between wanting to succeed, and wanting to avoid failure.

Quite often a desire to avoid failure is motivated by a fear of failure. Fear of failure itself is not a bad thing. Some of the most prominent athletes suggest that fear of failure is a hugely powerful motivator. For example, in a fascinating interview by Chris Broussard of ESPN Magazine[2], LeBron James (winner of four NBA Most Valuable Players awards and two Olympic Gold Medals) talks about fear of failure: "That's one of my biggest obstacles. I'm afraid of failure. I want to succeed so bad that I become afraid of failing." When asked how he deals with this fear, he remarked, "Just win [laughs]. Keep winning and I don't have to worry about it. Keep winning." Notice, he doesn't say "don't lose"; he says, "keep winning".

But a fear of failure can be destructive if it causes you to *focus* on that potential failure, especially in the lead-up to highly important performances. William Shakespeare said that, "Our doubts are traitors, and make us lose the good we oft might win, by fearing to attempt"[3] and it is this point that is at the heart of what we are saying here.

If fear of failure encourages avoidance, withdrawal, or a 'fear to attempt', then how are we supposed to fulfil our potential? In contrast, if fear of failure encourages an unshakeable focus on success, meticulousness in our preparation, and persistence when things get tough, then it is possible to perform to, and beyond, our expectations. This can be more simply expressed using the Figure below:

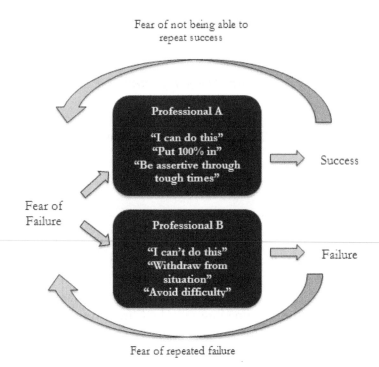

Fear of not being able to repeat success

Professional A

"I can do this"
"Put 100% in"
"Be assertive through tough times"

Success

Fear of Failure

Professional B

"I can't do this"
"Withdraw from situation"
"Avoid difficulty"

Failure

Fear of repeated failure

We see a lot of fear of failure in our consultancy work with elite athletes and coaches. Because fear of failure is rife, so too are avoidance goals. An avoidance goal incorporates a desire and an intention to avoid mistakes, often accompanied by "don't mess up" type statements alongside the over-thinking of performance.

Research has shown that athletes who harbour avoidance goals such as "I want to avoid performing worse than others" actually perform worse - even if they react to that situation in a challenge state![4] That is, although a challenge state is hugely beneficial for performance, if you have a high-level of avoidance goals you are still at risk of falling short of your performance expectations. Avoidance goals are very powerful indeed.

One of the key pieces of advice we offer to athletes performing at the very top level is to focus only on the things they need to do to perform well, particularly in the moments leading up to their performance. In other words, direct your focus towards what you want to achieve (success), rather than what you want to avoid (failure). In contrast to an avoidance goal, an approach goal encompasses a desire and an intention to execute the skills you have control over and are confident in performing.

Approach Goal: "In this game I am going to try to be consistent with my second serves."

Avoidance Goal: "In this game I am going to try not to be inconsistent with my second serves."

Even though both types of goal are ultimately about achieving something (e.g., being consistent with second serves), there is a huge difference between the two goals in terms of how they influence behaviour and performance.[5] Individuals who adopt approach goals are more likely to face up to difficult situations, prepare well for the big event, persist when things get tough, and are much more able to go into performance situations feeling positive.[6] Further, those who focus on approach goals interpret meaningful situations as a challenge - look back at chapter 2 for a refresher on the challenge state.

Approach goals are linked with a challenge state and effective coping under pressure.

In contrast, individuals who adopt avoidance goals are likely to withdraw from difficult situations, underprepare for the big event, seek escape when things get tough, and go into performance situations feeling negative and defensive. Further, those who focus on avoidance goals interpret meaningful situations as a threat.

As you can imagine, a confident individual who feels in control of their performance, and who also has an approach focus, is much more likely to fulfil their potential as indicated by The MAPP. So in the previous example (second serves) we can see that this goal is controllable by the tennis athlete, relies on self-confidence to make it happen, and is focused on the desired outcome, rather than the outcome to be avoided.

Take Usain Bolt (Olympic sprint Champion who holds both the 100 metres and 200 metres world records) for example. A man not short of self-confidence or success, and who is able to focus on what he needs to do to succeed despite having known 'weaknesses' (relative to his opponents). Bolt says that, "For me, I'm focused on what I want to do. I know what I need to do to be a champion, so I'm working on it." Although he realizes he is not the best straight-out-of-the-blocks, he focuses on what he can do better than anyone. Finish. "There are better starters then me but I'm a strong finisher."[7]

Approaching Performance

He who is not courageous enough to take risks will accomplish nothing in life.[8]

Muhammad Ali, Boxer

Courage is not so much about being able to deal with pressure without fear of failure or potential embarrassment; it is more about dealing with pressure *despite* fear of failure and potential embarrassment.

Having the courage to approach your performances is largely about dealing with the nerves that precede them. If we can get past apprehension, we can feel free to express ourselves fully. Unchecked and untamed, anxiety is the serial killer of opportunity. So how can we learn to overcome those feelings of doubt and unease we often experience when making tough decisions? Or the nerves and trepidation we may have when we know that this moment is a decisive moment in our careers? How can we develop the freedom to express ourselves in our endeavours? How can we learn to approach instead of avoid?

There are a number of strategies you can use to harness your approach goal focus involving thinking and behaving in the right way. In this chapter, we will drill down into what you can do in the moments leading up to that important event, performance, or competition, to ensure you are always focused on the things that will maximize your performance.

The greatest mistake you can make in life is to continually be afraid you will make one.[9]

Elbert Hubbard (19th century American writer, publisher, artist, and philosopher)

Think The Right Way: Overthinking

How the hell are you gonna think and hit at the same time?[10]

Yogi Berra, Baseball Player

Elite athletes are extremely skilled at what they do. Most are often able to perform their skills without thinking, like they are on autopilot.

Consider driving for a moment. When you get in your car you are about to endeavour upon an extremely complicated and complex process involving the coordination of mind and body to perform intricate movements safely and proficiently.

Chapter 7

If you have been driving for some time, no doubt you perform these intricate movements without thinking about the precise processes your body and brain goes through to produce them. Maybe when you were learning to drive this wasn't the case. When learning to drive you probably focused on how to produce these skills to make sure you were being accurate. Each movement was intentional and deliberate. But now you are skilled in driving, and have developed expertise, these movements can be made without having to process each component. In fact, you are able to talk, sing, think about your day, and even navigate (unless you have GPS in which case you will be listening to that intently!)

But if we told you that you had to take your driving test again to be able to continue driving - to try to make sure your performance is flawless - you will probably abandon this automatic process and instead break the skill down into its component parts. Are my hands in the right place? Have I checked my mirrors? Am I in the right lane? When do I indicate? The trouble is, by breaking the skill down, you are now performing in a way that is very odd to your brain and body. You are an expert, remember, and all of this intricate skill knowledge is not needed anymore. So what is normally a smooth and proficient performance becomes an uncoordinated mess. You overthought it.

Sport psychologists have recognized for a long time that one of the main reasons athletes choke under pressure is because they overthink skill execution. By choking, we mean that your performances take a sudden and dramatic nosedive compared to your normal functioning due to perceived pressure. To illustrate, in sport overthinking is problematic. Performance is so important in that potentially career-changing debut match that many athletes take extra care to do the right things, at the right time, in the right way. Herein lays the problem. You know how to perform, and you know what your core skills are, but when overthinking these elements you actually disrupt the mechanics of those skills. So you end up doing things you don't want to do, and stuttering with your skills, with your performance looking unnatural.

Overthinking well-rehearsed and learned skills under pressure leads to underperforming at the big event.

Professor Sian Beilock of the University of Chicago is a leading expert on this phenomenon and calls it "paralysis by analysis."[11] Beilock's work has shown how, when under pressure, overthinking can destroy performance in tasks that would normally be quite easy.[12] This is worrying because we spend so much time honing those sport skills and it could all be undermined by being unable to deliver our skills when it matters the most. Fear not, research has also found some powerful strategies that counteract paralysis by analysis. Let's take a look.

Think Simple

Overthinking is so common because, when the going gets tough, we want to make sure we have got all of those little component parts right. When working with athletes suffering from paralysis by analysis, the aim is to help them simplify their thoughts into a single focus - moments before the execution of a skill.[13] This single focus should be relevant to the activity being attempted. For example, a golfer may use some key 'swing thoughts' that direct the action of the swing without being too prescriptive. For example they might use the word "smooth" as they approach a drive, or "nice n easy" when putting. You can do the same with your performance activities.

So let's take making your first team debut in front of packed home stadium, for example. Making a good first team debut is important for your career development and you can read hundreds of books about how to perform, execute your skills, behave, deal with mistakes, boost your confidence, hydrate… the list goes on. All valuable information that should be considered when approaching a game of this importance. However, in that moment, as you walk from the changing room, down the tunnel towards the pitch hearing

155

the noisy home crowd, seeing your opponents, can you really focus on all of that stuff and still function as a complex human being going into a complicated and pressured performance environment? Probably not. So instead, you can grab all of that important 'first team debut' stuff you need to do and bundle it into a neat package and give it a label. This label should be a) meaningful to you, and b) an obvious indication as to what it's for. A useful label might be "assertive" or "confident" or could even be a word that relates to somebody who you wish to emulate or model in this situation, such as "My hero" or "The General".

Remember, this is all about making a good first team debut, which in the context of professional team sports is largely about how you behave. Confident, composed, and assertive actions lead to confident, composed, and assertive performances, which make a good debut.

You can apply this principle to any performance situation you are faced with. Just bundle the component parts and give that package of actions and thoughts a meaningful label. *Simplify* the complexity of performance under pressure.

Don't Say Don't

We see it so often. You are the person of choice for your team when it comes to taking kicks for goal (including free kicks and penalties), and once again you are called upon to deliver accurate and successful kicks in an important forthcoming soccer match. You can be relied on to successfully execute your kicks in the most challenging of situations.

It's the day of the soccer match and as you practice your kicking routines prior to the match for the last time, and prepare, you feel nervous, this is an important match for you and your team. Your manager says three simple words to you that have been the curse of many an athlete: "Don't mess up". These words ring and echo in your mind as you walk onto the pitch in front of the supporters, "Don't mess up, whatever you do," you say to yourself. In injury time at the end of the match, one of your teammates is brought down for a foul just outside the penalty area. You have a free-kick opportunity which is in a part of the pitch that you prefer. The match is evenly poised, and the scores level at 1-1. This is your chance to win the game for your team and send your supporters into ecstasy. As you stand ready at the end of your free-kick run-up, you remind yourself, "Don't let the moment get to you, whatever you do don't mess up". Then you begin your run-up and deliver a poorly executed free kick with the ball ballooning way over your opponent's goal. The referee blows the whistle for the end of the match. You emerge from the pitch bemused in the midst of disappointed looks from your manager and team. "What happened?" you ponder.

The above is probably enough to give some of you nightmares. In fact, it was anxiety-provoking even writing it! But it is quite common to see failure snatched from the jaws of victory because, at the crucial moment, one's focus turns to potential failure because of a simple "don't" statement.

One of the most popular avoidance goals we hear from athletes is "Don't mess up" or "Don't fail". There are a huge variety of peoples' "don'ts" but typically they reflect the exact occurrence the person wants to avoid. For example, prior to an important golf putt many golfers say to themselves "Don't leave it short" or even worse "Don't miss". You see, when under pressure the brain doesn't really understand the word "don't". Oddly, "don't" means "do" when we are stressed.

Surely in highly important performance situations it makes perfect sense to tell yourself not to fail, or not to do the things that would undermine your performance? Unfortunately, the late Daniel M. Wegner, former Professor of Psychology at Harvard found that telling yourself not to do something actually and ironically increases the likelihood of doing it. He famously used the white bear thought experiment[14] to illustrate this inconvenient truth, in which we are told not to think of a white bear, an impossible task because as soon as the bear enters our minds - trying to erase it is futile. Try it for yourself. Don't think of a white bear. Whatever you do don't think of a white bear.

Thinking of a white bear? Don't feel too bad, its human nature! Professor Wegner found that these "*ironic processes*" are more likely to occur when you are anxious, which is bad news for performance because pretty much everyone experiences some degree of anxiety when approaching an important event. In his book *White bears and other unwanted thoughts* Professor Wegner explained that:

"The need for mental control probably would not occur to us if we had no worries or problems... We attempt mental control primarily when we have the feeling that something is wrong or soon will be... This happens all too often, for it seems unwanted thoughts can arise from many possible sources. If we are concerned about an upcoming event, if we cannot get over something that happened a while ago, or if we cannot seem to make ourselves behave as we wish, we will probably have unwanted thoughts lurking about."[15]

But why, when we tell ourselves not to do or think about something, does it ironically increase the likelihood of doing (and thinking about) that thing? The answer has to do with the way your mind works under pressure. The attempt to not think about, or do, something triggers two simultaneous mental processes:

1. A conscious process (in your awareness) where you search your mind and your surroundings for items consistent with the intended goal state (e.g., the fairway on a golf course).

2. An unconscious process where you ensure any threats (e.g., the water or bunker at either side of the fairway) are noticed and handled.

The difference between one and two is not as simple as 'good' and 'bad'. The second process is crucial for us to function in everyday life, as the ability to recognize threats can save our lives and stop us from making literally fatal mistakes in some contexts (e.g., deciding when to cross the street when traffic is free flowing).

But in performance situations, when we are anxious and our mental resources are being used up by worry and concern, this second unconscious process takes charge. You see, because the first process is a *conscious* one, it needs some resources in order to work properly. If these resources have been stolen by anxiety, the process fails. Because the second process is an *unconscious* one, it is not affected by anxiety and thus has free reign over our focus of attention. Therefore your ability to focus on aspects that will help you perform is impaired, and your ability to focus on aspects that will lead to failure is enhanced.

*Avoid ironic processes. Avoid the use
of 'don't' statements and focus on things
you need to do to perform well.*

So, circumstances where your mind is full of worry (especially), or
when you are feeling pressured, sees ironic processes take over,
leading you to think and act in ways that are directly opposed to your
goals. With athletes we work with we demonstrate this effect by
having them not think of a white bear, or pink elephant, for 60
seconds (under time pressure). During this task we ask them to mark
a piece of paper every time they *do* think of a white bear or pink
elephant. In one minute, it's very hard for them to get the unwanted
thought out of their heads and they are astonished at their inability to
complete this task successfully. There are usually numerous marks on
the paper.

Then, after some time, we ask the client to think about whatever they
want for a further minute. Interestingly, the white bear emerges
again. Suppressing the white bear actually makes the image stronger
and more persistent in the mind (this is known as the *rebound effect*).
But there are ways to combat this unfortunate mental process. Next
we will detail some tried and tested strategies that can combat ironic
processes in those all-important performance situations.

What White Bear?

Think of a red car.

The difficult thing about trying to combat ironic processes is that
they are natural and important mental functions, therefore effort is
required to shut them down.

One of the best ways to combat ironic processes is by making sure
that your focus is fully fixed - like a laser - on the things that you
want to do in that performance. That is, only focus on the things you

need to do to perform well. Keep that first mental process (the conscious one) at full strength and help it to search for items consistent with your intended goals.[16]

In other words, if producing a fluent and proficient opening drive off the tee in golf is your goal, then focus only on doing that and not on the consequences of not doing so.

In the thought experiment where we encouraged you not to think of a white bear, people fail in this task because they are so focused on not thinking about the white bear. People are more successful if they are given an alternative to focus on. We have used a red car for this purpose, in line with Professor Wegner's work. So instead of merely not thinking of a white bear, we encourage the person to think of a red car when they have the urge to think of a white bear. The white bear still crops up every now and again.

Later, when we ask the person to spend a minute thinking about anything they want - the white bear is likely to pop into the mind from time to time, but much less frequently. Replacing the white bear with a red car lessens the effects of ironic processes.

The white bear/red car has implications for preparing for your big performance. When those unwanted thoughts crop up in your mind, which they surely will, replace them with images and thoughts of what you need to do to succeed. To make sure you are able to do this, *plan* your thoughts so that when an unwanted thought crops up, you have a *ready* replacement for it.

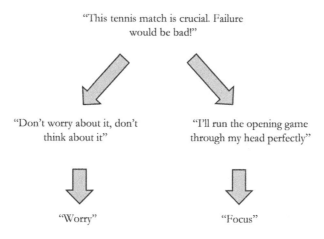

So, in performance situations, instead of trying not to think of potential failures, visualize yourself doing the things you need to do to perform well. This might involve running the opening moments of your performance over in your head, or seeing yourself delivering your skills confidently and assertively. While it is extremely difficult to completely rid the mind of potential negative consequences, being able to focus only on what you need to do is one of the best ways to limit the effects of ironic processes.

Empty Your Head

In chapter 6 we talked about using the 'Empty your Head' strategy to deal with negative thoughts in the lead-up to your performance. Here we apply the same technique to combat ironic processes. Instead of trying not to worry, or trying to suppress concerns about a performance, it is more beneficial to express these worries and concerns. Indeed, supressing worries and concerns can lead to worrying more about that event, and can also negatively affect sleep quality.[17] By expressing these unwanted and negative thoughts you are removing the need to suppress them. So in performance situations you are less likely to experience a rebound effect (this is when the supressed thought crops up later just when you don't want

161

it to) because you have not supressed any unwanted thoughts in the first place.

To express your unwanted thoughts, write them down. Write down exactly what is on your mind on some paper: your fears and concerns, the negative consequences and all. Then read what you have written, rip the paper up, and throw it in the bin. Other similar strategies include using expressive writing techniques such as writing short stories about your worries and also writing funny poems about them. Research suggests that this can reduce the invasiveness of unwanted thoughts and feelings of anxiety. By not suppressing those unwanted thoughts, you are taking power away from ironic processes.

Be Ironic to Fight Irony

As discussed above, with ironic processes - one trick is not to suppress your thoughts, but to let them flow into your head and play-out unrestricted. However, there is an important rule you need to follow. It would be unwise to let unwanted thoughts run free on the day of your performance, or even the night before. Instead, make time in the days leading up to your performance to *think about* potential failure and even let your mind drift back to past failures.

As you think, you may experience a couple of things. First, you may start to realize that, actually, it wasn't as bad as you first thought and that you were able to cope with the setback anyway. After all, despite your previous failure, you are still here participating in your sport and competing and have probably learned a lot from the experience. You might even remind yourself that your heroes and role models have failed on their way to success and although you might have failed many times - you have survived.

Second, by thinking about the unwanted experience, that is, by exposing yourself to an outcome that you want to avoid, you may actually fear that outcome less. As mentioned previously, this is known as *desensitization* and we will talk more about it in chapter 9. In essence, because you are making yourself think about the thing you fear, you learn not to fear it. The negative consequences swirl around your head and not one of those consequences involves dying(!). By accepting that failure happens and by allowing yourself to think about unwanted outcomes, you remove the need for thought suppression and therefore remove ironic processes.

With strategies to combat ironic processes, there is a common theme. Take time and effort to process the unwanted thoughts you may have about your performance and do this in a controlled and structured manner. Each of the strategies involves letting your unwanted thoughts breathe, while employing either distraction (e.g., red car) or expression (writing them down or imagining them) techniques. Don't fight a losing battle with your mind. Unwanted thoughts can be resilient so instead of supressing them, embrace and deal with them.

Create and Take Opportunities

You miss 100 percent of the shots you never take.[18]

Wayne Gretzky, Ice Hockey Player

If an American football player wants to score more touchdowns, then one of the key pieces of advice offered is to put himself or herself in more scoring positions. It sounds obvious. But success in sport is largely to do with creating and taking opportunities. After all, how can you take a touchdown opportunity if you never make one? Often, focusing on success is about being there, putting oneself in a position to succeed, creating and seizing the moment. It is less about thinking and more about doing. You may be highly confident, and you may feel composed under pressure, but how can you turn these mental states into effective performances? By making and taking chances.

Many athletes think that, one day, they will be tapped on the shoulder by the head coach or the coach of their national squad with the good news that their potential has been spotted and they are being offered an amazing new contract or have been selected to play for their country. This rarely happens. It is unrealistic to sit around waiting for opportunities and wondering when you will be noticed for your hard work and intelligence. It is much more productive and controllable to have an open and honest conversation with your coach and the coach of your national team as to your aspirations and career intentions. Often, when we work with athletes who are stuck in a rut and have stagnated, we ask what opportunities they have sought from their line manager or coach. What have they been doing this year to improve themselves as an individual? How many times have they requested a meeting with their manager or coach to talk about their progression? How many extracurricular activities have they done recently? Typically, the answers to these questions are negative.

In most high level sport performance environments it is not enough to work hard and wait for somebody to notice your endeavours. It's much more productive to be upfront with your superiors, whether it's your manager or coach, and let them know what you have done, what you are doing, and what you intend to do - to help you and your team achieve its objectives.

From a behavioural point of view, adopting an approach focus instead of an avoidance focus is really quite simple (in theory). It's about realizing what it takes to get to the next level, and working towards that vision. Along the way you may need to have some difficult conversations, and have to do and say things that are uncomfortable and new. You may have to learn some new skills and sometimes ask 'stupid questions'. But by putting yourself in a position to succeed, you are more likely to achieve your goals.

Adopting an approach focus can be quite simple.
It's about realising what it takes to get to the
next level, and working towards that vision.

We did some work with an athlete who had a secret desire to become captain of his team when the old captain retired. After the coach had chosen his captain, the athlete came and spoke to us and expressed his disappointment at not being chosen. However, not once had the athlete told the coach that he wanted to be captain. Not once did he tell the coach what he had done to make him the best person for the role. He had never intimated his leadership goals to anyone. The coach thought the athlete had great leadership skills but thought he didn't want to be captain as he had never talked about it.

On talking to the athlete further, it emerged that he had not taken these important steps because he was concerned that once his desires were known, and if he was then overlooked for the captaincy, it would be embarrassing and more difficult to accept. He stopped himself from expressing his desire for the role because of fear of failure, and as a result didn't get the role! Coaches and managers are not mind readers.

Avoidance goals can manifest within unhelpful and destructive thoughts, but can also cause complete withdrawal from difficult situations so that failure can be avoided. Psychologists call this *self-handicapping* and it means that failure can be better tolerated if you didn't put 100% into that performance situation. In other words, by withdrawing effort you protect your ego by saying, "It's not that I have poor leadership skills, it's because I didn't ask for the captaincy role that I was overlooked" or "I was unsuccessful at that trial game because I didn't try hard, not because I wasn't the best player" or "If I don't put in 100% effort, or I don't have that conversation with my coach about my aspirations, then if I fail it's because I did not commit, not because I do not have the ability to go to the next level".

Self-handicapping works! That is, it is effective at preserving your ego and protecting you from low self-esteem. But, self-handicapping is not the trait of a successful person and it will not help you to fulfil your potential. As we saw with Cristiano Ronaldo in chapter 6, success comes from continual hard work, so withdrawing effort - even to protect your ego - should not be a part of your performance strategy.

The Big First Three

Concentrate all your thoughts upon the work at hand. The sun's rays do not burn until brought to a focus.[19]

Alexander Graham Bell (inventor of the first practical telephone)

As we have written many times in this book, it is important to focus *only* on what you need to do to perform well in the moments leading up to your performance. Just before you start your run-up, get into the starting blocks, walk to the plate, stand over the putt, or lead your team - thoughts of failure are useless. In the moment it is more productive to give your mind some really simple things to focus on. Importantly, these things should be performance relevant, and potentially helpful for performance. Having some simple images and thoughts to focus on - directly prior to performance - will stave off paralysis by analysis, ironic processes, and negative self-talk.

Also, by making these images and thoughts performance-relevant and helpful, you are more likely to enter that performance in the right mindset to fulfil your potential.

One of the most effective ways that athletes can focus only on what they need to do is by focusing on something we call the *big first three* things they want to do in the first 3-4 minutes of their performance. Let's take a recent example with a rugby player.

The rugby player in question was having trouble settling into matches. He was struggling to find that moment in performance when he had calmed down and the jittery nerves had dissipated. Thinking about, and visualizing, three important activities when the game began was needed to get him settled into the game. These were:

1. Make that first pass a positive one

2. Make that first tackle a hard one

3. Make that first block a solid one

The importance of this strategy was two-fold. First it helped the player to focus and concentrate on a small number of achievable targets instead of worries and concerns about the match, and second it meant that once the big three targets had been achieved it helped to foster *momentum* by raising self-confidence. Put simply, the athlete told his body what he wanted it to do in those first crucial minutes of a match. Each time he met a target, he got a shot of self-belief and settled into the match more.

What do I mean by concentration? I mean focusing totally on the business at hand and commanding your body to do exactly what you want it to do.[20]

Arnold Palmer, Golfer

We have used this strategy with many athletes, across different sports, who all have different targets. The important thing is that the targets are indicative of performing well and the targets are *achievable* early on in the performance. The targets should be controllable by the athlete and should be focused on *doing something*, not avoiding it. Take your next big event into consideration and create your own *big first three* targets. Maybe it's an important event or competition. Once you have arrived at your big three, ask yourself the following four questions:

A. Is each one necessary for performing well?

B. Is each one achievable early on in the performance?

C. Is each one controllable by me?

D. Is each one focused on approach goals?

You should aim to answer yes to all four questions. For example, some *big first three* targets, recommended for a tee shot on the first hole in the past, have been:

1. Nice assertive body language on the tee box

2. Positive decision making for where you choose to aim your shot

3. Flowing execution of your pre-shot routine

All are an important part of preforming well. All are achievable early on in a round of golf. All are controllable by you. All are focused on doing something rather than avoiding something.

The big first three aids focus on performance-related information.

Once you have developed your three targets, the next step is to commit to them with an intention to make them happen on the day when it counts. This involves making sure that, as part of your pre-performance routine, you focus only on these three targets in the direct lead-up to the event. This is usually in the couple of minutes before you start your performance and it should include trigger words and visualization.

For example, you could visualize yourself meeting those three targets, triggered by a cue word (e.g., "positive"). It also involves ensuring that your intention to meet those targets is reinforced by a plan. You may also wish to include an implementation intention ("if-then") here too (from chapter 6). For example, "If I complete my three targets, then I know I am on the way to performing well."

The Challenge Strategy

Focusing on success is not just about conquering paralysis by analysis, combatting ironic processes, and creating and taking opportunities. It is also the amalgamation of what we covered across chapters 5, 6, and 7.

Focusing on success is about maintaining self-confidence and control when it matters most so that you can direct your energy towards the things you know you can do and the things you know you can control. When working with athletes this is known as *The Challenge Strategy*, because it brings together the resources of self-confidence, control, and approach goals to get you into a challenge state when it matters most. We know that, in The MAPP, having high and maintained resources leads to effective performance. The Challenge Strategy should be used in the lead up to your performance right from your morning preparations, through to your journey, and to directly before your performance.

The first step with The Challenge Strategy is to develop specific routines for each of the three resources (self-confidence, control, approach goals). We hope that the content of chapters 5, 6, and 7 have provided you with ample material to draw from in this regard. The best way to develop your routines is by trying the techniques covered thus far and understanding, for yourself, which ones fit your way of preparing for your situation.

The Challenge Strategy comprises the resources of self-confidence, control, and approach goals.

The template below will help you to structure your Challenge Strategy. In the box (Technique), write down what technique you will use to enhance that resource. Then in the larger box (Details), add some details about what the technique involves in terms of when and where it will be employed, and the content. Then give your Challenge Strategy a name (Name) to identify its purpose. In the grey box (top-right) write down which of the three resources you are bolstering by using the strategy.

My Challenge Strategies

Name:	
Technique:	
Details:	

Name:	
Technique:	
Details:	

Name:	
Technique:	
Details:	

Some "Challenge Strategy" Examples

Name: My Opening Game Strategy	Self-Confidence
Technique: Visualization of my best possible start to a tennis match	
Details: Visualization will include seeing myself delivering consistent and effective first serves. My strokes are flowing and accurate. I will visualize this performance in the changing room prior to the match in real-time and in great detail.	

Name: My Opening Game Strategy	Control
Technique: Empty my head	
Details: The night before my match, before I go to bed, I will write down my worries and concerns about the competition and spend 10 minutes dwelling on those thoughts. Then I will rip up the paper and throw it away.	

Name: My Opening Game Strategy	Approach Goals
Technique: Think simple	
Details: Directly before my match I will remind myself to be "commanding, confident, and energetic". I know that lots of other aspects fit within these skills, but I know how to do them and I just need to jog my mind as to how I want to perform.	

Chapter 7

Brief Summary

Together with chapters 5 and 6, chapter 7 has introduced you to the importance of focusing on success. That sounds easy right? But when the pressure is on, and in the face of adversity, it can be extremely difficult. You might start to over-analyse a situation, start to tell yourself "don't mess up", and may start to withdraw effort through fear of failure. Tackle these thoughts and behaviours head on.

Chapter 7 has helped you to develop skills that can prevent destructive thoughts and actions, and has guided you in the development of strategies that enhance your approach goals for performance situations. As with all you have learned so far in this book, practice is key here. Practice and use your Challenge Strategies. Adapt them to new situations. Alter them as you develop further in your career. The skills you have learned in chapters 5, 6, and 7 are very much 'life skills' that will serve you well throughout your sporting endeavours.

Next, we will move on from resources and look at how you can regulate the way your body and mind react in pressure situations, and how you can harness bodily reactions for maximal performance when it matters most.

Most Important Point

Success comes to those who focus on what they need to do to perform well, instead of focusing on what could go wrong.

---

[1] Babe Ruth quote (n.d). *Sport psychology quotes*. Retreived on August 19, 2014 from, https://sportpsychquotes.wordpress.com/tag/fear/

[2] Broussard, C. (2013). The King James version. *ESPN The Magazine*, Oct, 28th 2013. http://espn.go.com/nba/story/_/id/9824909/lebron-james-michael-jordan-fear-failure-35-point-games-more-espn-magazine

[3] Shakespeare, W., Mowat, B. A., & Werstine, P. (2005). *Measure for measure.* London: Simon and Schuster.

[4] Turner, M. J., Jones, M. V., Sheffield, D., Slater, M. J., Barker, J. B., & Bell, J. (2013). Who thrives under pressure? Predicting the performance of elite academy cricketers using the cardiovascular indicators of challenge and threat states. *Journal of Sport and Exercise Psychology, 35*, (4), 387-397.

[5] Chalabaev, A., Major, B., Cury, F., & Sarrazin, P. (2009). Physiological markers of challenge and threat mediate the effects of performance-based goals on performance. *Journal of Experimental Social Psychology, 45*, 991-994. doi: 10.1016/j.jesp.2009.04.009

[6] Jones, M., Meijen, C., McCarthy, P. J., & Sheffield, D. (2009). A theory of challenge and threat states in athletes. *International Review of Sport and Exercise Psychology, 2*, 161-180. doi: 10.1080/17509840902829331

[7] Usain Bolt quotes (n. d.). *In brainyquote.com.* Retrieved May 21, 2014, from http://www.brainyquote.com/quotes/authors/u/usain_bolt.html#L27ko VxfFlydk8c0.99

[8] Muhammad Ali biography (n. d.). *In IMDb.* Retrieved May 21, 2014, from http://www.imdb.com/name/nm0000738/bio

[9] Elbert Hubbard (2014, April 18). *In wikiquote.org.* Retrieved May 21, 2014, from http://en.wikiquote.org/wiki/Elbert_Hubbard

[10] Yogi-isms (n. d.). *In umpirebob.com.* Retrieved May 21, 2014, from http://www.umpirebob.com/DATA/yogiisms.htm

[11] Beilock, S. L. (2007). Choking under pressure. In R. Baumeister and K. Vohs (Eds.), *Encyclopaedia of Social Psychology.* Sage Publications.

[12] Beilock, S. (2010). *Choke: What the secrets of the brain reveal about getting it right when you have to.* New York, NY: Simon and Schuster.

[13] Liao, C., & Masters, R. S. W. (2001). Analogy learning: A means to implicit motor learning. *Journal of Sports Sciences, 19*, 307-319.

[14] Wegner, D. M. (1989). *White bears and other unwanted thoughts: Suppression, obsession, and the psychology of mental control.* New York: Viking/Penguin.

[15] Wegner, D. M. (1994). *White Bears and Other Unwanted Thoughts: Suppression, Obsession, and the Psychology of Mental Control.* The Guilford Press: NY, New York.

[16] Wegner, D. M. (2011). Setting free the bears: escape from thought suppression. *American Psychologist, 66*, (8), 671-680.

[17] Guastella A. J., & Moulds M. L. (2007). The impact of rumination on sleep quality following a stressful life event. *Personality and Individual Differences, 42*, (6), 1151-1162. doi:10.1016/j.paid.2006.04.028

[18] Wayne Gretzky (2011, July 5). *In philosiblog.com.* Retrieved May 21, 2014, from http://philosiblog.com/2011/07/05/you-miss-100-percent-of/

[19] Alexander Graham Bell (n. d.). *In wikiquote.com.* Retrieved May 21, 2014, from http://en.wikiquote.org/wiki/Alexander_Graham_Bell

[20] Arnold Palmer: Quotes from the king (2013, September 10). *In yourgolftravel.com.* Retrieved May 21, 2014, from http://www.yourgolftravel.com/19th-hole/2013/09/10/arnold-palmer-quotes-from-the-king/

Chapter 8: Self-Regulate

Adopting the right attitude can convert a
negative stress into a positive one.[1]

Hans Selye, 20th Century Austrian-Canadian scientist who pioneered the study of stress

It's not stress that kills us; it is our reaction to it.[2]

Stress is good.

Hold on to that thought for a moment. Think of all the times in sport when you have been under pressure and have felt uncomfortable, sweaty, shaky, dry-mouthed, and nauseous. These symptoms seem bad, right? Well the truth is that these symptoms are neither good nor bad; they are merely bodily responses telling you that something important is coming up and you had better get ready for it. If you are able to hold on to the idea that these reactions are helpful, are a sign of your body preparing for action, and that - actually - stress is good, you are on your way to being able to regulate your emotions effectively and maximise your own potential and performance.

The skill of reinterpreting your emotional responses, such as stress, as 'something helpful' is really the pinnacle of self-regulation. As the quote from Hans Selye suggests, you can convert negative stress to positive stress by adopting the right attitude. Many elite athletes actually appraise stress in a positive manner. They believe that their physical and mental symptoms, associated with an up-and-coming performance, are actually useful and just part of their preparation. Of course, if these thoughts and feelings become uncontrollable then performance suffers. One only has to recall many of the performance meltdowns that have occurred in elite sport over the years. Take Roberto Baggio for example; Baggio won the Silver Boot (second highest goal scorer) at the 1994 Soccer World Cup, but is mostly remembered for missing the decisive penalty against Brazil in the final. Or the golfer Greg Norman, who built an impressive 6 stroke lead at the 1996 Masters, before shooting a 78 on the final day, losing the green jacket to Nick Faldo by 5 strokes. Or more recently, Team New Zealand, who were 8-1 in front of the USA in sailing's prestigious America's Cup, but then lost 8 races in a row to lose 9-8 overall. These pressure-induced meltdowns give us an understanding of how appraising stress in a negative way can interfere with performance.

In this chapter we present the idea that you can decide how to interpret symptoms of stress and can therefore react positively to these signs (instead of dreading them and using them as an opportunity to panic).

This chapter is about how you can regulate your physiological and emotional reactions to stressful situations in sport. Some of this chapter will include guidance on reducing the intensity of physical symptoms, some of it will be about increasing the intensity of physical symptoms, so that you can exercise control over your reactions. But eventually we will arrive at the skill of interpreting stress symptoms as beneficial, helping you to adopt the philosophy that *stress is good.*

I used to love the games but I used to feel sick before them because I was so nervous, it was a horrible feeling.[3]

Wayne Rooney, Footballer

Being able to see stress as a good thing probably seems a tad utopian. Getting to the point where you can honestly view stress symptoms as helpful is tough and takes a lot of adaptation (more about this in chapter 9). So in this chapter we will first introduce you to some practical skills that you can learn and use to take charge of your body in crucial performance situations. Some skills are easy to learn, some are difficult, but mostly these skills draw on your ability to carry out evidence-based sequences to either relax or activate the body.

The pinnacle of being able to self-regulate is about seeing stress as helpful.

For example, perhaps prior to an important golf round you are fidgety, unsettled, with your heart racing and hands shaking. You may want to help your body to relax so that you can face that round with calm and poise. Then again, maybe you feel the opposite. Maybe you feel tired, heavy, flat, not ready. Here you may want to help your body to get activated so you can face that round with vigour and energy. The ability to change and control the way you feel is about self-regulation, and helping you to relax or activate, when you need to, is the first step. So this chapter is really divided into three parts:

A. Relax

B. Activate

C. Re-interpret

An Aside About "Biofeedback"

Biofeedback is prominently used in the athletic setting to help athletes measure and regulate their arousal levels (e.g., heart rate and breathing rate) in real-time.[4] Further, biofeedback is based on the principle that individuals can voluntarily control their stress levels. It essentially involves monitoring biological responses that are usually inaccessible, using electronic equipment such as a heart rate monitor or even a brain scanner. The individual receives feedback from an instrument measuring aspects of a stress response and then experiments with different techniques to regulate the stress response.[5] Eventually, the person can self-regulate without the aid of these instruments.[6]

For example, relatively easy-to-use technology can be used to measure key signs of arousal such as heart rate, blood pressure, respiration rate, and respiration depth. For the purposes of this chapter, heart rate is going to be our focus.

Heart Rate

Heart rate (as the name suggests) tells you how fast the heart is beating in Beats Per Minute (BPM). Put simply, heart rate is a great indicator of how relaxed or activated you are. The faster your rate, the more aroused you are.

Heart rate automatically speeds up and slows down in line with your arousal level – it's involuntary. So if you want to feel relaxed the night before your big sporting event, or want to feel at ease in the lead up to the event, monitoring your heart rate at choice times will enhance your ability to self-regulate. It is because biofeedback is so useful at regulating arousal that athletes who perform target sports (shooting, archery, etc.) find tremendous gains in their accuracy when a calm, steady mind and body is present.

You have to slow your heart rate, stay calm. You have to shoot in between your heartbeats.[7]

Chris Kyle, ex-United States Navy SEAL

When trying the techniques we talk about in this chapter, we suggest you have access to a heart rate measuring device (there are lots of free mobile phone Apps that measure heart rate through the camera on your smart phone).

*Heart rate is a good indicator of how
relaxed or activated you are.*

When you become skilled at controlling your heart rate, then do away with the heart rate monitor, confident in the knowledge that you can relax at a moment's notice. In other words, the ability to control stress levels in a controlled environment can be transferred to actual performance situations. If you don't have access to a heart rate monitor – no worries! You can still get tremendous gains from what we cover in this chapter.

A. Relax

I just try to relax and think about video games, what I'm gonna do after the race, what I'm gonna do just to chill. Stuff like that to relax a little before the race.[8]

Usain Bolt, Sprinter

One key aspect of self-regulation is learning the skill of relaxation. Indeed, in sport where training and competition takes up most of your time, many athletes have neglected the skill of relaxation to help them deal with the stresses of sport. While interpreting stress as positive is seen as the best way of dealing with pressure and tough situations, there are times when being able to relax is vital.

You have to block everything out and be extremely focused and be relaxed and mellow too.[9]

Jennifer Capriati, former World Number 1 tennis player

As the above quotes from Jennifer Capriati and Usain Bolt suggest, being able to relax when you need to is an important skill. The techniques we cover here can, of course, be used whenever you want, but we will focus on approaching important performance situations. In this section we outline four key strategies to facilitate relaxation:

1. Muscle Relaxation

2. Focused Breathing

3. Centering

4. Self-Hypnosis

1. Muscle Relaxation

Muscle relaxation training helps you to reduce stress and tension, and also promotes a more positive mind-set. This is known as *body to mind relaxation*, in that you are focusing on relaxing the body, which then helps the mind to relax as well. Muscle relaxation was pioneered by American physician Dr. Edmund Jacobson in the early 1920s.[10, 11]

Typically, athletes undergoing muscle relaxation try to 'let go' and try not to focus on any thoughts at all. This technique works best with daily practice. Remember, in our lives it is not normal for us to experience such deep relaxation in the face of stressful situations, therefore a lot of work needs to be done by you to program your body differently.

The procedure

There are many versions of muscle relaxation. Some are very long and comprehensive. Some are short and are applicable in short timespans when relaxation needs to be achieved quickly. But, in general, muscle relaxation involves tensing and relaxing progressively larger muscle groups starting from the top of your body and working down, or from your toes and working up. This is what Dr. Jacobson called "Progressive Muscular Relaxation" or PMR. During muscle relaxation you should focus on the different feelings associated with tension and relaxation. That is, really try to concentrate on the tension when the muscle is tensed, and really try to focus on the lack of tension when the muscle is relaxed. Like any skill, muscle relaxation requires training before it can have a beneficial effect on your stress levels prior to sport events. Therefore, we encourage you to practice the muscle relaxation programme detailed in this chapter daily for 10 minutes over a week and monitor your progress using biofeedback (your heart rate monitor).

The tensing of each muscle group should last for a count of five seconds, followed by a real focus on relaxing that muscle group for five seconds. Do this three times for each muscle group before going on to the next. As mentioned previously, before you begin this procedure make a note of your heart rate. Then, after you have completed the procedure, have a look at your heart rate again. This will provide important biofeedback information and allow you to gain confidence that this skill is indeed relaxing your body (evidenced by a decreased heart rate).

After a week's practice you will notice an improvement in your ability to self-regulate and begin to see the value of integrating muscle relaxation into part of your preparation for important performance situations, or alternatively as a integral part of your daily sport-related routines.

*Progressive muscle relaxation relieves tension and helps
to create an awareness of the different feelings
between tension and relaxation.*

Step by Step Progressive Muscle Relaxation

For the initial practices of your muscle relaxation, find a place where you are comfortable and unlikely to be interrupted. You can lie down, but typically people sit upright in a chair with their backside pressed against the back of the chair and their feet a shoulder width apart. In our experience, this procedure works best if you audio-record the scripted procedure (below) onto a CD, MP3 player, or smartphone and listen to it. Usually, athletes we work with will read the script out aloud while audio-recording their voice onto their smartphone. By doing this you can then listen to the procedure at any time and can close your eyes while you listen, which helps to internalise the process so you don't have to struggle to remember the progression. So relax, and go through the procedure below:

Close your eyes and relax your whole body:

1. Tense the muscles in the lower part of both legs by curling up your toes. Hold that tension for 1, 2, 3, 4, 5 - now relax focusing on the feelings of relaxation for 1, 2, 3, 4, 5 – Repeat three times.

2. Tense the muscles in your thighs - hold that tension for 1, 2, 3, 4, 5 and now focus on the feelings of relaxation for 1, 2, 3, 4, 5 – Repeat three times.

3. Clench both hands by making a fist. Hold the tension in your hands for 1, 2, 3, 4, 5 and now relax focusing on the feelings of relaxation for 1, 2, 3, 4, 5 – Repeat three times.

4. Take a deep breath, lift your rib cage as high as you can and now relax by exhaling 1, 2, 3, 4, 5 – Repeat three times.

5. Try and push your shoulders back into the floor or chair. Hold that tension for 1, 2, 3, 4, 5. Now relax, focusing on the feelings of relaxation 1, 2, 3, 4, 5 – Repeat three times.

6. Tense your neck muscles by shrugging your shoulders - hold the tension for 1, 2, 3, 4, 5 and now relax focusing on the feelings of relaxation for 1, 2, 3, 4, 5 – Repeat three times.

7. Now tense your facial muscles, your forehead, jaw, and the muscles around your eyes, and mouth. Hold the tension for 1, 2, 3, 4, 5 and relax. Focus on the feelings of relaxation for 1, 2, 3, 4, 5 – Repeat three times.

8. You should now be feeling more relaxed; feel how calm your mind and body are.

2. Focused Breathing

It's one of the keys. Without emotional control, you cannot play... you cannot react. You have to know what you have to do... You have to be cool.[12]

**José Mourinho,
Football Manager**

We have all heard the phrase "take a deep breath" when faced with a tough situation and many of us may recall David Beckham taking a deep breath before his penalty kick for England against Argentina at the 2002 soccer World Cup. Learning to control your breathing will have an impact on your physiological stress response. In fact, deep breathing, or diaphragmatic breathing[13] to use the correct terminology, maximizes the amount of oxygen that goes into the bloodstream via the lungs.

This is an effective way of triggering the body's normal relaxation response. Focused and controlled breathing has a direct impact on cardiac output meaning less variability in heart rate and blood pressure and regulated oxygen uptake.

Essentially, concentrating on (and slowing down) your breathing can help you to reduce unhelpful stress responses, including worry and anxiety, and stay calm prior to and during important performance situations. We encourage you to practice the technique for 10 minutes every day for one week in conjunction with the progressive muscular relaxation procedure we have just covered. Maybe practice focused breathing when travelling to training or walking the dog. Then you can integrate it into preparation for performance events or daily routines. With practice you will be able to relax using *only* a couple of deep breaths which will enhance the effects of muscle relaxation and can be used when you need to relax rapidly. Remember to monitor your heart rate whilst undertaking focused breathing, as this will provide important biofeedback information and allow you to gain confidence in the skill.

Breathing procedure

In the initial practices of your focused breathing find a place where you are comfortable and unlikely to be interrupted. It is important that, while you are breathing in and out, you breathe deeply from the abdomen, getting as much air as possible into your lungs. One way of making sure you are inhaling from the abdomen is to place a hand on your abdomen and make sure it rises as you inhale. Place the other hand on your chest to make sure it does not rise as you inhale. You can inhale more oxygen by breathing from your abdomen rather than your chest. More oxygen means less tension and more relaxation. To begin, sit comfortably with your back straight. Put one hand on your chest and the other on your stomach. Now follow the step-by-step process below:[14]

1. Breathe in through your nose. The hand on your stomach should rise. The hand on your chest should move very little. *Count in, two, three, four.*

2. Exhale through your mouth, pushing out as much air as you can, while contracting your abdominal muscles. The hand on

your stomach should move in as you exhale, but your other hand should not move much. *Count out, two, three, four.*

3. Breathe in through your nose... *in, two, three, four.*

4. Exhale through your mouth ... *out, two, three, four.*

5. *In, two, three, four.*

6. *Out, two, three, four.*

Repeat this breathing process as many times as you are able to, or as many times as you need. Typically this would be 10-15 minutes when practicing. We recommend you use the heart rate monitor and note down your heart rate prior to the procedure and then afterwards to see the impact of the breathing on your arousal levels. Then, gradually reduce the amount of time you spend on the procedure and again assess your heart rate. As you become more skilled you will be able to lower your heart rate in 10 minutes, then 5 minutes, and if you become highly skilled it may only take a minute.

Learning to breathe rhythmically and effectively will aid relaxation and promote positive stress reactions.

---

3. Centering / (Centre-ing)

You have to be able to center yourself, to let all of your emotions go... Don't ever forget that you play with your soul as well as your body.[15]

**Kareem Abdul-Jabbar,
Basketball Player**

Have you ever watched Jonny Wilkinson's ball kicking routine in rugby, and wondered what he was doing cupping his hands like he was trying to crack open a nut? Well, in essence, he was engaging in a process called *centering* which is crucial prior to, and during, performance to stay focused, avoid distractions, and stay grounded.

Centering is actually a technique that originated in Aikido, a Japanese martial art. Aikido is nonviolent and translates as "the way of unifying life energy". Centering will help you to stay in the moment and release past and future thoughts, worries and plans, and hence alleviate stress. Centering allows you to pay attention to your body and breathing, redirecting your focus from negative thoughts or anxiety-causing events to the present task or situation.[16]

---

*Centering promotes self-awareness and encourages
one to gain control of one's stress response.*

Similar to focused breathing, centering involves focusing on the rate of breathing and maintaining a slow, steady pace. During performance it may be important for you to gain quick control of your stress response. Like any skill, centering requires training before it can have a beneficial effect on your emotions and performance. Therefore, we encourage you to practice the technique for 10 minutes every day for a week before integrating it (before and during performance). As before, use biofeedback to measure your response and gain confidence in the skill.

Centering Procedure

We would advise that you first undertake the breathing procedure we have just covered *before* centering. Also, remember that centering is about managing energy so make sure you also engage in positive thinking whilst undertaking it. Perhaps draw from chapter 5 and give yourself some positive self-talk. As with the previous techniques in this chapter, follow the procedure step by step:

1. Stand with your feet apart and knees bent slightly with your weight evenly distributed between your two feet. This is about finding your physical centre of gravity which is commonly just below your waist. Remember where your centre is - as this part of your body stabilizes you.

2. Relax the neck and shoulders with your mouth slightly open to reduce the tension in your jaw muscles.

3. Breathe in through your nose and push your stomach out. As you do so, focus on two things: your stomach moving out, and maintaining the relaxation in your neck and shoulders.

4. Exhale slowly through your mouth and feel your stomach muscles relaxing and your body pressing down to the ground.

5. Repeat this process five more times.

6. Focus on the feelings of relaxation.

Now it may have occurred to you that undertaking this exercise in front of a roomful of teammates prior to a match may cause you to appear a little odd. We would advise that you conduct your centering in a private space. Many people find it useful before they leave the house for a big game, or they find a private space in their training environment to spend a minute centering themselves. It's important to remember that whichever relaxation strategy you choose to adopt, it should be practical and usable in the context in which you wish to use it.

4. Hypnosis and Self-Hypnosis

We have all heard of, or seen, hypnotherapists wielding their magic wands as they evoke power and control over people; typically, because of these experiences, the term 'hypnosis' is shrouded in misconception, myth, and apprehension. But what actually is hypnosis and how can it be used to help us self-regulate?

First, the term 'hypnosis' implies an interaction between one person (the hypnotist or practitioner), and another person or people (the participant/client or group of participants). Through such an interaction the practitioner attempts to influence the participants' thoughts, perceptions, feelings and behaviour by prompting them to focus on ideas, thoughts and images that intend to facilitate long-term behavioural change.

Typically, to induce such a condition, a practitioner uses verbal communication in the form of 'suggestions' (i.e., words, phrases, metaphors) to bring about changes in the aforementioned thoughts, feelings, perceptions and behaviour. For example, an athlete suffering with low levels of self-confidence about distance running, after a long-term injury, would be presented with positive suggestions focused on thoughts and feelings about successful running performances before injury.

Hypnosis can perhaps be best described by recalling how one would feel just prior to falling asleep (indeed the term "hypnosis" is derived from the Greek word "hypnos", which means "sleep"). Typically in this situation one is calm, relaxed and may experience vivid thoughts and images as well as inadvertent twitches in the arms and legs. To recreate this, hypnosis usually commences with the use of relaxation techniques.

Once an individual is relaxed, suggestions are presented that focus on the desired cognitive or behavioural change (e.g., to be more confident and take on challenges). In a relaxed condition the mind is more susceptible to change as the conscious mind can be bypassed and therefore allow communication with the unconscious part of the mind, where traits and habits are found to occur.

Data from our own sport psychology laboratory and data collected in other domains (e.g., psychotherapy, dentistry) shows that hypnosis is very effective in bringing about *positive* changes in thoughts, feelings, and behaviours, along with actual sport performance.[17]

There is evidence supporting the use of hypnosis with regards to pain reduction, asthma, skin disorders, smoking cessation, weight loss and psychiatric problems. Hypnosis is consistently used to aid depression, anxiety disorders, and to increase self-confidence. A number of elite sports people have successfully used hypnosis to aid them in their preparation or to overcome a particular performance-related problem such as pre-competitive anxiety. For example, Tiger Woods used hypnosis when he was younger to help get into the right mindset for golf performance.[18]

To give an example, we worked previously with a professional soccer player who approached us with low-levels of self-confidence, having lost his position in the team. After eight hypnosis sessions, which focused on increasing self-confidence, motivation, and enjoyment, the athlete felt more confident and enthusiastic about his performance, and himself in general. He regained his position within the team, was given the team captaincy, and was voted player of the season by his teammates.

In short, hypnosis is not magic or trickery, and research shows how beneficial it can be in regulating mental states and aiding performance. However, unless you happen to know a hypnotist, or are willing to invest in one, you are probably unsure how all of this interesting information about hypnosis applies to you. Well, hypnosis does not necessarily have to be a one-way street. You can help yourself by using *self-hypnosis*. Self-hypnosis, or 'autohypnosis', is a self-administered hypnotic state. In fact, many scientists and practitioners maintain that because during hypnosis you accept the suggestions made to you by a hypnotist, you are actually hypnotizing yourself anyway.[19]

In practice, self-hypnosis[20] enables individuals, in their own time, to rehearse hypnosis procedures (e.g., deep relaxation) and present themselves with suggestions (e.g., confidence, control, and approach goals).[21]

---

*Hypnosis combines relaxation,
imagery, and suggestion(s).*

The benefit of self-hypnosis is that it can be used directly before those all-important performances when (and where) one may feel it appropriate. For example, self-hypnosis can be used to reduce stress levels and reinforce affirmations (e.g., believing in your ability) whilst preparing to compete in that all important monthly golf medal.

Self-hypnosis has an important role as part of a pre-performance routine (or during a performance routine) as outlined in chapter 6.

You can take time to go through a structured process to deliver suggestions to yourself, thus taking control of your preparation in a very powerful way. For example, whilst working with an elite curler for a number of years we developed a self-hypnosis script which was recorded using their own voice onto an MP3 player; prior to a match they would find a quiet area and listen further to the suggestions.

While we obviously cannot hypnotise you using this book, we recommend you use the principles of hypnosis to develop your own self-hypnosis script for use before performances. Again, record your heart rate before and after self-hypnosis. Follow these steps to conduct your self-hypnosis:

1. Figure out what you want to gain from self-hypnosis. If you want to enhance your self-confidence then plan some self-affirmations to use for when you are deep in the self-hypnosis process. This should be based on your visualization ammunition and may include something like "You have done it before so you can do it again", for example.

2. Get relaxed. You can use the techniques we already talked about here such as progressive muscular relaxation with focused breathing. Remember to find a comfortable place where you will not be disturbed. 20 minutes should do it so make sure you have time, as there is nothing more un-relaxing than a stringent time limit!

3. 'Walk down the steps'. When you are fully relaxed, start to imagine that you are at the top of a flight of stairs. There are 10 steps and as you descend each step you get more and more relaxed. Tell yourself that as you walk off the final step, you will be in deep relaxation with nothing on your mind but that fact.

4. Enjoy it. Stay here for a while, in this deeply relaxed state. You may feel like you are floating; if so, navigate the space you find yourself in.

5. As you drift, start to use the self-affirmations that you authored before you embarked on this self-hypnosis. We recommend using 4-5 well thought out and powerful statements that increase feelings of confidence, control, motivation, and enjoyment. You can be very general with

these, or they can be related to a specific upcoming performance. Repeat these self-affirmations over and over.

6. Walk up the steps. Each step you ascend - you feel more alert and awake. Do this slowly and meaningfully. Focus on the feelings of climbing each step and the increased sense of awareness you get from ascending. When you get to step 3, you should be ready to take the last few steps being fully alert and ready to open your eyes.

7. Awake. Once you have fully ascended the stairs, give yourself a moment to slowly open your eyes. It may help to imagine a door at the top of the stairs where, as you open and walk through it, light floods your vision. Open your eyes and reorient yourself with your surroundings. As you come back to reality, remind yourself that you are awake and alert.

8. Carry the effects with you. The self-affirmations can be used as triggers at any time after this self-hypnosis. These triggers can be used to evoke positive thoughts and feelings for performance at any time.

B. Activate

Relax? How can anybody relax and play golf?
You have to grip the club, don't you?[22]

Ben Hogan, Golfer

Many athletes talk about being flat before they perform and instead of wanting to calm down, they want to get energized for their performance. Stress can cause people to feel tired before the big event, which can hinder their performance as they don't feel switched on or ready. Or sometimes, athletes are required to perform in a competition that is not particularly motivating, and they really struggle to get up for it. This phenomenon is part of the reason underdogs can cause upsets in sport – how can the world number 1 get up for a match with the world number 100?

Activation techniques can be used to counteract lethargy for performance, so you can control how pumped you feel for that big event. Thus, in stark contrast to the relaxation techniques we have just covered, this next section introduces three key activation techniques:

1. Activation and Coping Imagery

2. Music

3. Psyching up

1. Activation and Coping Imagery

One strategy that is effective in activating a positive stress response in performance situations is that of imagery. But it is important to use a specific type of imagery here. In chapter 5 we talked about using imagery to increase confidence, but here we are talking about using imagery to *increase* heart rate and arousal (activation) so that you feel pumped for a performance.[23, 24]

Remember, imagery works best when it is realistic and vivid, so that you can recreate the mental and physical responses to a specific situation. So to get pumped for performance you can visualize yourself performing in a forthcoming situation with all its intensity. Importantly, you see yourself coping with the situation and thriving under pressure. This prepares the mind and body for what it is about to do. It energizes the brain to focus on performance and activates the body for assertive and confident behaviour.

As with all the skills throughout this book, imagery requires a period of training before it can have a beneficial effect on performance. With this in mind have a go now while using a heart rate monitor. This biofeedback will indicate your ability to get energized for performance. Try to relax and get to resting levels. Then start to imagine going into that crucial upcoming situation and coping with it. Make it intense and realistic. After a minute, check your heart rate, it should have increased from rest indicating an increase in arousal.

Remember, some arousal is necessary for some people to perform and can be a very good thing indeed!

Developing an activation and coping imagery script

You are now going to develop an activation and coping imagery script. First, write down an upcoming situation or event that you think will be particularly stressful. This might be a training game, an important trial, or an end of season cup final. Now we want you to begin by providing as much detail as you can about the situation. Try and outline where the event might take place, how you might feel, the thoughts you may have, and what you have to do. It is important to provide as many elements as you can here.

Now you have this information you can begin to compile your script which you will then begin to practice. The example below will provide an outline of how to develop an imagery script. Once you have written your script, it can be recorded onto an MP3 player and you can listen to it when required. People normally listen to their imagery script as close to the event as possible, but it makes more sense to memorise the imagery script so that you can get activated directly before any performance situation. .

In addition, this coping imagery script also has a beneficial effect on other psychological factors. For example, by seeing yourself cope, self-confidence will increase and so too will your focus on success. So, in your script, make sure you take the opportunity to build in some confidence boosting images from your visualization ammunition in chapter 5.

Example of a sprinter's coping imagery script for an athletics meet

You are sitting in the holding room - waiting for the call from one of the event organisers to come and get you for the 100m final.

As the event organiser walks into the holding room and calls you and the other competitors forward – you stand up and feel strong and powerful, your body language is positive and assertive and your head is held high; you look at your opponents in a dominant manner. In this moment you feel your body rush with energy telling you that you are ready for this.

As you walk out onto the athletics track and walk over to your starting block you look around and immediately recognize faces from the crowd. These people are very important to you and you want to impress them. You feel good about this as all the right people are there to see you perform well in this pressured situation.

You take your place near the blocks and run the race through your head. From start to finish you see the whole race in your mind. You take some rythmic breaths and remind yourself that you are ready for this. You approach the blocks and settle into your starting posotiion, still picturing the race you about to run. You await the gun and hear nothing but silence.

See yourself reacting positively to the sound of the gun, responding with composure and grace. This is your time and you have control over the situation. You process the transitions of the 100m and you are pleased with how your mind and body react, you cross the line and realise that you have won the race and achieved a PB. Stay in the moment for a while. This demanding situation in which you have coped well is playing out in your head. Remind yourself that this is where you want to be and that you are ready for this challenging test.

2. Music

I listen to hip hop and rap to sort of help me get focused, to get ready to get up and do what I'm there to do. It helps me to tune everything out, and take one step at a time. I always have on my headphones to block out all of the other distractions and I'm just focused on doing the best that I can.[25]

Michael Phelps, Swimmer

As you are probably aware music can be emotional, motivating, confidence-building, and relaxing. With these outcomes in mind it is no wonder that music can help you to achieve the appropriate stress response needed for performance.

In the quote above, Michael Phelps talks about how music helps him to get focused, and this is a very common way to use music in sports. Indeed, you may have noticed at the 2012 London Olympics that most swimmers had headphones on as they entered the aquatic centre to compete. It's just a part of what they do, their routine, to get into the right frame of mind and the right physiological state for high-pressure performance.

Many people listen to music as a distraction, but music can be used, very specifically, to create and evoke certain thoughts and feelings. It is likely that you have had experiences of listening to music that triggers a particular memory or feeling. You can use this to your advantage for performance.[26] You can select certain songs or types of music to trigger certain feelings that can activate the body.[27]

To achieve the appropriate mindset for performance it is important to select a song (or series of songs) that make you feel energetic and ready to go. Typically, but not exclusively, athletes we have worked with will opt for fast-paced music to get them activated. Alternatively, the music you choose could be of a certain genre (e.g., heavy metal, drum n bass, hip hop).

Assertive lyrics are powerful too, so it's not just about the type or tempo of music. You should consider selecting songs that contain words or phrases that match the mindset you are trying to achieve. One of the most popular songs for athletes is 'Lose Yourself' by Eminem[28] which contains highly inspiring 'against all odds' type lyrics. Conversely, a soccer athlete we worked with listened to bagpipes on the journey to performance venues as it evoked strong patriotic memories of home (Scotland).

Whilst, in general, we would encourage you to avoid music that brings about negative emotions such as sadness or anger, these emotions may be helpful if the situation requires you to be assertive or particularly passionate about something. For example, harnessing anger may be helpful if you feel that you can use this energy to exert authority over a group of individuals. Boxers will often use anger to create the intensity they need to perform. Similarly, sadness can be used to help deliver information that requires sensitivity and empathy.

But for activating your body and mind for performance, we recommend music that is positive and motivational. The precise reason why certain music is able to regulate activation is still under debate, but evidence tells us that listening to fast-paced music (e.g., drum n bass) increases the levels of cortisol, growth hormone, and norepinephrine in the blood, which are consistent with heightened nervous system activity.

Dr. Mona Lisa Chanda and Dr. Daniel J. Levitin, scientists at McGill's Laboratory for Music Perception, Cognition, and Expertise, suggest that the brainstem interprets music as a signal related to our survival and, as such, can influence our physiological reactions.[29] For example, fast paced, loud, sudden music mimics sounds in nature that are related to an alarm call, and it is this music that is stimulating and activating. On the other hand, soft, low-pitched sounds which build in volume as time passes mimics maternal vocalizations such as purring and cooing, and it is this music that relaxes and calms.

Music is a useful and powerful technique to promote helpful reactions to stress. Be sure to choose your playlist wisely!

Remember to monitor your heart rate whilst listening to different types of music; this will provide important biofeedback information alongside allowing you to identify the most appropriate type of music. As with previous techniques in this chapter, get yourself nice and relaxed, then listen to your choice and think about the up-and-coming event that you want to perform well in. Check your heart rate after a couple of minutes. You should see it increase if your music is activating you sufficiently.

Developing a playlist

Think of your activation playlist as an E.P. Not quite an album's worth of material, but a bit more than just a single. It should be a collection of tracks that share a common thread – the common thread here is that all of the tracks should be positive and motivational, typically fast-paced and beat-heavy. Think of it like a concept E.P. – a bit like your very own mini-Sgt Pepper's by The Beatles.

You can listen to the tracks from start to finish if you have time before your performance, or you can select one track if you only have a brief amount of time prior to performance. The key is that you specifically identify tracks for the sole purpose of activating yourself for performance. The tracks then function as a trigger when you hear them – elevating your heart rate and shifting more energy and oxygen to your brain and body. Experiment with your playlist and try to arrive at the best activation playlist possible. Choose four tracks, and for each, identify the name of the track, the artist, and importantly, your main reason(s) for selecting the track:

My playlist

Track #1

Name of Track:

Artist:

Reason for choosing it:

Track #2

Name of Track:

Artist:

Reason for choosing it:

Track #3

Name of Track:

Artist:

Reason for choosing it:

Track #4

Name of Track:

Artist:

Reason for choosing it:

3. Psyching up

Before you play, you have to get yourself in the right frame of mind. If you're not mentally right, you won't be able to produce your best. Everyone's different though – you have to do what works for you. Some guys run around shouting and screaming whereas others prefer to chill out.[30]

Lewis Moody, Rugby Player

Psyching up is about using a cluster of powerful psychological and behavioural techniques to let the brain and body know that the time is now - to get ready for performance.[31] As mentioned previously, many athletes we have worked with complain not that they are too activated for performance, but exactly the opposite, that they are not activated enough; many find these techniques easy to learn and master. Also, psyching up is quick to apply in performance situations. Some of these techniques are simply the opposite to what you would do to relax, and some are skills in their own right.

Intense breathing

Remember, rhythmic and controlled breathing is a great relaxer, so it stands to reason that non-rhythmic and uncontrolled breathing would cause the opposite effect. So prior to your performance take several hard exhalations. Then take some heavy breaths in and out.

This is most useful directly before performance when you need your energy to be at its highest.

Be energetic

There is no greater cure for lethargy than acting how you want to feel. In this case move your body to get the heart pumping to your muscles and, even more importantly, your brain. Remind the body that it's time to get ready and give your heart a kick-start. Physical activity increases heart rate and cardiac output (the amount of blood pumped from the heart), which means that you can get blood to the areas that need it for your performance. A great example of an athlete using his body to psych themselves up is Rafa Nadal. Here, Nadal describes his approach to facing Roger Federer:[32]

"I stood up and began exercising, violently — activating my explosiveness... I jumped up and down, ran in short bursts from one end of the cramped space to the other — no more than six metres or so. I stopped short, rotated my neck, my shoulders, my wrists, crouched down and bent my knees. Then more jumps, more mini-sprints, as if I were alone in my gym back home. Always with my earphones on, the music pumping inside my head."

Nadal also talks about taking a cold shower before the match, saying that, *"I'm a different man when I emerge. I'm activated. I'm in 'the flow', as sports psychologists describe a state of alert concentration in which the body moves by pure instinct, like a fish in a current. Nothing else exists but the battle ahead."*

So walk around, shake your arms, jump, do some shadow boxing... anything to give your body a kick-start. As you may recall from chapter 6, Mo Farah drinks some espressos to get himself feeling pumped for a race.

Talk a good game

Using self-talk that is arrogant and complacent will make the body react in a relaxed manner. Why get activated and pumped for a performance if it's in the bag already?

Also, if you are not confident and feel that you are fighting a losing battle, your body will give up too. So here it is important to make sure your self-talk uses fighting language mixed with motivational and confidence boosting words and phrases. Remind the body that you need it to get up for this performance because it is important. For example, you may use phrases such as: "It will be tough but I know I can do it", "I am ready for this challenge", or "This is my time to show what I can do". You may even wish to distil these phrases into some short cue phrases such as "fight", "challenge", or "my time".

The above mental and physical techniques are best applied together so you can give your mind and body a boost before you perform. Again, try them out and monitor your heart rate so you can be sure they are having the desired effect.

Do it

Throughout this chapter, we have encouraged you to use a heart rate monitor to assess the effect of the different strategies on how fast your heart is beating. We have found that one of the most effective ways to help professionals regulate their heart rate, and therefore their activation, is to simply *focus on their heart rate monitor*.

To explain: after a period of training when we introduce athletes to the techniques described in this chapter, we then set a task to either decrease or increase heart rate. But to do this the athlete has to keep a constant eye on their heart rate reading on the monitor. What we find is that those who are well-trained in relaxation and activation techniques are able to self-regulate easily, and astonishingly, are unable to tell us exactly how they do it.

You see the best way to self-regulate is to use a mixture of the techniques we have covered in different ways. By focusing on your heart rate and setting yourself the task of lowering it (or increasing it) you will find that you are able to do it in your own unique way that encompasses lots of different strategies. It doesn't matter what method you use as long as you are able to self-regulate when it matters most (If you are interested in finding out more about this fascinating skill, read Mario Beauregard's excellent book: Brain

Wars). We reiterate the Bruce Lee quote from the preface of this book: "Only use that which works".

C. Re-interpret

Say what you want… the brain is used to being scared. So it's always alert. It's like a tiger in the forest afraid that somebody is coming out, and if somebody is coming out, Yah! Then you bite! But you must be ready.[33]

Luciano Pavarotti, Opera Singer

The above quote is from a fascinating mini-documentary about stage fright in which Luciano Pavarotti beautifully described how he felt about the anxiety he experienced before performing. Singing can be massively affected by performance anxiety, and the ability of the performer to turn that stage fright into a memorable performance is about transferring that energy into something useful. Many singers talk about the nerves they feel before a performance being an extremely important part of their preparation, to the extent that if the stage fright was not present, performance would actually suffer. This is similar in sport, as many athletes experience stage fright about competition, but see this as a good thing for performance. A great example of this is Alan Hansen, one of the most successful British soccer players of all time. In a fascinating book by Joe Sillett and Karl Morris, Hansen talks about his pre-match anxiety:[34]

"I was always terrible beforehand. It's a bit like broadcasting, where the nerves are always there beforehand. I've never been nervous on a football pitch in my life but beforehand, I was like a nervous wreck. Going down the tunnel was like a release. All nerves disappeared… The nerves were unbelievable. I was thinking we might get beaten, we might play badly, we might struggle; everything and anything which was negative. But the great thing was that when I got on the pitch, all I thought about was winning… The fear of losing was obviously good for me; the fear of getting beaten actually helped me."

201

As we said at the beginning of this chapter, and as Alan Hansen talks about above, stress is good. Stress might *feel* bad, but can help your performance. The symptoms of stress are neither positive nor negative, they are merely bodily responses telling you that something important is coming up and you had better get ready for it. If you are able to truly recognize that this is the case, stress can be extremely beneficial. In fact research into challenge and threat (see chapter 2 for a reminder of this area) has shown that reinterpreting anxiety symptoms as helpful can lead to a challenge state and help performance in important events.

We have spent a lot of time in this chapter introducing you to the many different ways to change your physical reactions to stress so that you can get into the right state for performance. These are valuable and very commonly used techniques across countless domains. But the most effective strategy we have used with athletes is *reappraisal*. Reappraisal is about the re-interpretation of physical reactions to stress as helpful for performance.

Reappraisal

Recent work by Dr. Jeremy Jamieson and colleagues at Harvard University has shown that reappraising stress symptoms leads to individuals interpreting their anxiety as helpful for performance, and therefore just like a self-fulfilling prophecy, performance is aided.[35]

The skill of reappraising stress symptoms as helpful is known as a *response-focused strategy* when you focus on altering what you think about how you react to pressure (rather than changing what you think about the situation itself).

Dr. Jamieson's research had students in the USA approaching an important exam (Graduate Record Examinations, or "GRE") consider their anxiety symptoms as helpful by telling them "recent research suggests that arousal doesn't hurt performance" and that "people who feel anxious during a test might actually do better".

The students were also encouraged to "simply remind yourself that your arousal could be helping you do well." The students who were encouraged to think in this way showed more efficient physiological reactions (similar to a challenge state) and perceived their anxiety as helpful. They were also more confident about the exam and actually performed better than students who were not encouraged to view their anxiety as helpful.[36]

Change what you think about how you react
to pressure, rather than changing what you
think about the situation itself.

You see, your anxiety response is functional, in that it prepares the mind and body for action, whether it's a penalty kick, a tie-break in tennis, or a cycling time trial. These stress reactions have helped humans to endure through millennia of evolution where the ability to quickly activate the body and brain at the first sign of danger has helped us survive tough and constantly changing conditions. Let's look at three very common symptoms of stress, and delve into why they occur and how they have helped us to survive:

1. Sweaty palms: Stress, anxiety, or excitement activate the sympathetic nervous system, increasing your heart rate, and also affecting the Eccrine sweat glands in your face, palms, the soles of your feet, and armpits. As a result of sympathetic nervous system activation, the sweat produced in the palms increases. Sweating when anxious helps control the humidity of the outer layer of the skin. In our evolutionary past, this would have aided hunting, fighting, and climbing by enhancing palm friction. In addition, sweat helps to cool the body for physical activity, so in preparation for an intense situation, body temperature is kept relatively constant(known as homeostasis).[37]

2. Muscle tension: Again, this is a result of sympathetic nervous system activation when anxious or excited. As part of our "fight or flight" response to pressure, noradrenaline signals the muscles to tense up in preparation for action. This helps

the muscles to ready themselves for rapid action in response to danger. In our evolutionary past, this would have aided escape from a predator, chasing of prey, or indeed battling predators. In your sport, you probably do not often have to evade predators or chase prey (in a literal sense), but you do engage in vigorous action (depending on your sport), so as you perform the muscles become less tense.[38]

3. Nausea: That pesky sympathetic nervous system has been at it again! Its activation releases hormones, including adrenaline, into the bloodstream to prepare the body for physical exertion. The stomach contains sensory nerves that are stimulated by this release of hormones and so butterflies and nausea occur. In addition, this release of hormones triggers the digestive system to shut down and release stores of fat and glucose (so we can use them for energy). In our evolutionary past, when evading a predator, there would have been little need for digestive function – this could wait until the ordeal was over.[39, 40]

So your body is trying to help you; it's not trying to trip you up. It is reacting automatically in a very complex and helpful manner, preparing you for action. If the anxiety response was of no use, as a species we would have probably got rid of it long ago. Also, if the anxiety response was not helpful, the tough and constantly changing environments that have shaped us would have led to our demise long ago. Of course, nowadays the dangers you face are dangers to your success or social standing (we call this *danger to esteem* – see The MAPP in chapter 2), rather than sabre-toothed tigers or woolly mammoths. The fact that we get anxious has, in part, made us successful as a species and therefore we should embrace this reaction more.

The aim of reappraisal is not to dampen or lessen the intensity of anxiety, but rather to reshape the anxiety as a tool we can use to help us achieve our goals. Or as Dr. Steve Bull (England Cricket Team psychologist and headquarters psychologist for three Olympic Games) puts it… "Nerves and butterflies are fine – they're a physical sign that you're mentally ready and eager. You have to get the butterflies to fly in formation, that's the trick."[41]

So next time you feel anxious about that upcoming performance, remind yourself that 'what you feel' implies that your body is getting you ready for this performance. Your body is trying to help you. You just need to let it.

Brief Summary

This chapter has taken you through some of the most powerful self-regulation strategies we use with athletes; strategies that are supported by a vast amount of research.

As with all skills, the strategies take time to learn and master, but when they are mastered they are extremely effective in helping to regulate how you react to pressure situations. We have also covered how anxiety is actually helpful as long as you view it as such. Some of the content in chapter 8 will pop up in our next chapter. Chapter 9 is about *adapting* to pressure and adversity, and it is all about toughening yourself so that, when the moment comes, you are able to fulfil your potential under the toughest of circumstances.

Most Important Point

Whether you want to feel relaxed or energized for performance, there are many techniques you can use to regulate how you feel. Remember, your stress response is there to help you, so use it!

---

[1] Watt, M. C. (2008). *Overcoming the fear of fear: How to reduce anxiety sensitivity.* Oakland, CA: New Harbinger Publications Inc.

[2] Berdik, C. (2013, March 10). How to make stress work in your favor. *The Boston Globe.* Retrieved May 21, 2014, from http://www.bostonglobe.com/ideas/2013/03/10/how-make-stress-work-your-favor/vMAvOIaegqFCFamQvS4DzN/story.html

[3] Ankers, G. (2011, October 13). Manchester United's Wayne Rooney admits he used to feel sick before Liverpool games. *Goal.com*. Retrieved May 21, 2014, from http://www.goal.com/en-gb/news/2896/premier-league/2011/10/13/2709011/manchester-uniteds-wayne-rooney-admits-he-used-to-feel-sick

[4] Examiner. (2013, November 5). Biofeedback for athletic performance. *Examiner*. Retrieved May 21, 2014, from http://www.examiner.com/article/biofeedback-for-athletic-performance

[5] Blumenstein, B., Bar-Eli, M., & Tenenbaum, G. (2002). *Brain and body in sport and exercise: Biofeedback applications in performance enhancement*. New York, NY: John Wiley and Sons Inc.

[6] Beauregard, M. (2012). *Brain Wars: The scientific battle over the existence of the mind and the proof that will change the way we live our lives*. New York, NY: Harper One.

[7] Life hack quotes. (n. d.). *In lifehack.org*. Retrieved May 21, 2014, from http://quotes.lifehack.org/quote/chris-kyle/you-have-to-slow-your-heart-rate/

[8] Usain Bolt Quotes (n. d.). *In brainyquote.com*. Retrieved May 21, 2014, from http://www.brainyquote.com/quotes/authors/u/usain_bolt.html

[9] Relaxed quotes. (n. d.). *In thinkexist.com*. Retrieved May 21, 2014, from http://thinkexist.com/quotes/with/keyword/relaxed/

[10] Jacobsen, E. (1929). *Progressive relaxation*. Oxford, England: University of Chicago Press.

[11] Jacobsen, E. (1938). *Progressive relaxation (2nd ed.)*. Oxford, England: University of Chicago Press.

[12] Mourinho's philosophy (n. d.). In *coachhiggo.wordpress.com*. Retrieved May 21, 2014, from http://coachhiggo.wordpress.com/2013/03/08/62/

[13] Varvogli, L., & Darviri, C. (2011). Stress management techniques: Evidence-based procedures that reduce stress and promote health. *Health Science Journal, 5*, (2), 74-89.

[14] A Harvard Medical School special health report. (2013). *Stress management: Approaches for preventing and reducing stress*. Harvard Health Publications.

[15] Basketball quotes (n. d.). In *sportsfeelgoodstories.com*. Retrieved May 21, 2014, from http://www.sportsfeelgoodstories.com/sport-quotes/sports-quotes/inspirational-basketball-quotes/

[16] Bradshaw, R. (1991). Stress management for teachers: A practical approach. *The Clearing House, 65*, (1), 43-47.

[17] Barker, J. B., Jones, M.V., & Greenlees, I. (2013). Using hypnosis to enhance self-efficacy in sport performers: Theory, research, and future Directions. *Journal of Clinical Sport Psychology, 7*, (3), 228-247.

[18] Gregory, S. (2010, April 5). Tiger at the Masters: An ultimate test of toughness. *Time.* Retrieved May 21, 2014, from http://content.time.com/time/business/article/0,8599,1977581,00.html

[19] Beauregard, M. (2012). *Brain Wars: The scientific battle over the existence of the mind and the proof that will change the way we live our lives.* New York, NY: Harper One.

[20] Scott, E. (2014, May 16). Using self-hypnosis for stress management. *About.com.* Retrieved May 21, 2014, from http://stress.about.com/od/tensiontamers/p/profilehypnosis.htm

[21] Power, M. (1976). *A practical guide to self-hypnosis.* California: Wilshire Book Company.

[22] Ben Hogan (n. d.). *In golftoday.co.uk.* Retrieved May 21, 2014, from http://www.golftoday.co.uk/noticeboard/quotes/ben_hogan.html

[23] Nordin, S. M., & Cumming, J. (2008). Types and functions of athletes' imagery: Testing predictions from the applied model of imagery use by examining effectiveness. *Imagery Types, Functions, and Effectiveness, 6*,189-200.

[24] Mellalieu, S. & Hanton, S. (2009). *Advances in applied sport psychology: A review.* New York, NY: Routledge.

[25] Time (2007, April 19). More questions with Michael Phelps. *Time.com.* Retrieved May 21, 2014, from http://content.time.com/time/arts/article/0,8599,1612765,00.html

[26] Ünal, A. B., de Waard, D., Epstude, K., & Steg, L. (2013). Driving with music: Effects on arousal and performance. *Transportation Research Part F: Traffic Psychology and Behaviour, 21*, 52-65.

[27] Husain, G., Thompson, W. F., & Chellenberg, E. G. (2002). Effects of musical tempo and mode on arousal, mood, and spatial abilities. *Music Perception, 20*, (2), 151–171.

[28] Eminem8MileVEVO (2011, September 20). *Eminem - Lose Yourself* (Clean Version) (Official). Interscope/Shady Records. Retrieved May 21, 2014, from http://www.youtube.com/watch?v=AF5WZ64bnIo&feature=kp

[29] Chanda, M. L., & and Levitin, D. J. (2013). The neurochemistry of music. *Trends in Cognitive Sciences*, *17*, (4), 179-194.

[30] Moody, L. (2005, May 9). Moody's loose forward guide. *BBC Sport*. Retrieved May 21, 2014, from http://news.bbc.co.uk/sport1/hi/rugby_union/get_involved/4201776.stm

[31] Taylor, J. (2010, May 7). The power of prime. *Psychology Today*. Retrieved May 21, 2014, from http://www.psychologytoday.com/blog/the-power-prime/201005/sports-psych-techniques

[32] Nadal, R. (2012). *My Story by Rafael Nadal with John Carlin*. London: Sphere.

[33] Uncjim (2007, December 30). Pavarotti and colleagues discuss stagefright. Retrieved May 21, 2014 http://www.youtube.com/watch?v=xJ_wnQM3P2w

[34] Sillett, J., & Morris, K. (2011). *Mentality*. West Sussex: Joe Sillett and Karl Morris.

[35] Jamieson, J.P., Nock, M.K., & Mendes, W.B. (2012). Mind over matter: Reappraising arousal improves cardiovascular and cognitive responses to stress. *Journal of Experimental Psychology: General*, *141*, 417-422.

[36] Jamieson, J.P., Mendes, W.B., Blackstock, E., & Schmader, T. (2010). Turning the knots in your stomach into bows: Reappraising arousal improves performance on the GRE. *Journal of Experimental Social Psychology*, *46*, 208-212.

[37] Scott. (2011, November 6). Why Your Palms Get Sweaty When You're Excited, Scared or Nervous. *Gizmodo.com*. Retrieved May 21, 2014 http://gizmodo.com/why-your-palms-get-sweaty-when-you-re-excited-scared-o-1459339958

[38] Muscular Symptoms of Stress (2014, July 18). In *stressdirections.com*. Retrieved May 21, 2014 http://www.stressdirections.com/content/view/44/66/

[39] King, R. M. (n. d). The Enteric Nervous System: The Brain in the Gut. *King's Psychology Network*. Retrieved May 21, 2014 http://www.psyking.net/id36.htm

[40] Hashworth1 (2011, July 18). Why do you feel sick when you're nervous? *Focus: Science and technology*. Retrieved May 21, 2014 http://sciencefocus.com/qa/why-do-you-feel-sick-when-youre-nervous

[41] Moss, W. (2008). *Make more, worry less: Secrets from 18 extraordinary people who created a bigger income and a better life.* New Jersey: Pearson Education Inc.

Chapter 9: Adapt

Charles Darwin, pioneer of the theory of evolution, famously observed that animals and human beings are not immutable. They have the ability to adapt and survive in the toughest of circumstances and environments, where typically only the 'fittest' prevail.

We are lucky. The course of evolution has instilled within us an amazing propensity to adapt to changing environments and situations, to acclimatize to tough and adverse conditions that test and try us. There are many examples throughout history of how people have adapted and demonstrated survival and development.

Curtis Jackson, also known as '50 Cent', was raised solely by his mother who worked as a cocaine dealer in a poverty-stricken neighbourhood. After some trouble with the law in his teens, he found hip hop and started recording music. On 24th May 2000, Jackson was shot 9 times at close range. He was shot in the hand, arm, hip, legs, chest, and face. He fully recovered in 5 months, and pursued his dream of becoming a successful rapper.[1] Marshall Mathers (aka Eminem) heard him, liked him, and he and legendary producer Dr Dre signed him for a reported $1m. Now Jackson is a musician, entrepreneur, investor, and actor, worth $270m.[2] Not only did he survive his past adversities, he thrived.

Chapter 9

There are many sport examples of athletes coming through adversity and thriving. One of the most extraordinary examples, that we take for granted these days, is Muhammad Ali's career.[3] After becoming heavyweight champion of the world in 1964, Ali (who was then known as Cassius Clay) announced that he had become a Muslim which was very bold at the time. In 1967 when he refused induction into the US army for the Vietnam War due to his religion, he angered many and was stripped of his world title and also his license to fight. This decision wasn't reversed until 1971.

In the same year, 1971, Ali lost to Joe Frazier – and then in 1974 he came back to beat Frazier. Ali then retained the heavyweight title (despite not being the favourite) in the famous "Rumble in the Jungle" after knocking out champion George Foreman in the eighth round. Although Ali was aging and was physically inferior to Foreman, he adopted the "rope-a-dope" strategy thus tiring and angering Foreman at which point Ali came off the ropes to knock Foreman out.

In 1978 Ali lost to Leon Spinks, but won back the title from Spinks just seven months later. After retiring in 1981, 1984 brought misfortune to Ali as he was diagnosed with Parkinson's disease. However, once again demonstrating his resilience, in 1996 Ali carried the Olympic torch to officially open the Atlanta Games. Ali is now considered one of the greatest athletes of all time and has been the recipient of countless awards for his humanitarian work (including the Presidential Medal of Freedom in 2005, the United States of America's highest civil award).

Only a man who knows what it is like to be defeated can reach down to the bottom of his soul and come up with the extra ounce of power it takes to win when the match is even.[4]

Muhammad Ali, Boxer

---

*Human beings have a great ability to learn to adapt to
all kinds of situations. It is in our DNA.*

Across the examples presented, the one overarching consistency is
that people in such situations were not born with the ability to thrive
in the face of adverse conditions. Indeed, we (humans) have
attempted to construct our world to be as comfortable as possible
(with varying levels of success). In other words, we do not want to
face adversity, but when we do, we *can* prevail.

The examples above evidence people who adapted to deal with their
situations, making use of environmental conditions, robust coping
resources, and social support from people around them. It is not that
you need to have had extremely unfortunate life-threatening
experiences to be successful in sport. The point is that we are capable
of enduring difficulties; an ability that can be developed, nurtured,
and harnessed.

Throughout this book we have helped you to harness your mental
skills in order to fulfil your potential when it matters most. This has
been achieved by changing and developing thought processes and
behaviours that we know bring about greater well-being and effective
performance. But an additional and often forgotten resource stems
from your naturally developed ability to *adapt* when placed under
significant situational demands.

The Free Throw

The free throw in basketball is a perfect example of having to
produce what is normally an easy skill for an elite basketball athlete
to execute but which under pressure becomes very difficult. Free
throws are usually given because of a foul by the opposing team. The
victim of the foul gets the chance to take a throw at the basket
unimpeded from 15 feet away. The conditions for a free throw are

always the same. The distance is always the same, the free throw is never impeded, and the basket is always at the same height. Pros can score these shots in training all day long, which makes missing them in pressured competitive games ever more interesting.

One investigation[5] looked at every regular season and playoff game in the NBA from 2003-2006 and analysed all free throws taken when the game was close (within 5 points between the sides). They found that compared to normal, players' free throw success took a dramatic drop when taking a free throw when their team was 1 point behind or 1 point ahead of the opposition. When the game is tied, players do better than normal in these shots. Players are at their worst when taking a free throw when their team is 1 point down. In fact, their free throw success drops by nearly 10%. Isn't that curious? Players choke only when they have a 1-point advantage or disadvantage – just when their team needs the points most.

There is something particularly intriguing about how top pros perform under pressure when taking free throws, which at first seems very counterintuitive. Research has shown that when the game is close, it is more difficult to score a free throw when you are competing at home rather than on the road. Athletes often talk about home advantage, but here we are talking about the exact opposite – a home disadvantage. One investigation[6] looked at basketball championship matches between 1967 and 1982 and the findings proved surprising. At crunch time, in the final game of a series, the visiting team were significantly more successful than the home team. The home team would typically choke when it came to free throws in the final game, but the road team performed as expected under such conditions. That is, it is not that the road team perform better – it is that the home team wilts under the pressure of free throws in the final.

A more recent investigation[7] of all NBA games from six seasons (2005-2010) revealed the same findings. Home teams perform better in general in free throws compared to the away team. But in clutch situations, when the free throw is highly important, the home team's free throw success plummets. When under pressure, performing at home actually damages performance compared to playing on the road. This completely reverses the notion of home advantage.

But what is so damaging about performing this simple skill in front of a home crowd when the game is on the line? It has to do with something called *self-focus* and is linked to 'paralysis by analysis' mentioned in chapter 7. You see, for the road team taking a free throw is quite different to taking one as the home team. For the road team, they must take the throw against a backdrop of shouts, jeers, and screams from the home crowd. These potential distractions can work in a player's favour when under pressure as they have to narrow their attentional focus to block out the crowd and focus only on hitting the target. However, the home team must take the free throw against the backdrop of silence and the weight of expectation from adoring home support. This causes self-focus. In an attempt to not let down the home crowd, players try to control every aspect of their throwing skills and focus on the mechanics of the movement, rather than simply taking the shot naturally.

As well as overthinking performance via self-focus, the athlete also has to contend with how their body reacts to the pressure of the situation. With so much on the line and with the fans watching and hoping for a successful free throw, it is little wonder the body and brain react with fear and distress that is completely unnecessary for the impending situation. Sweaty palms, muscular tremors, nausea, an irritable bowel, or a lump in the throat, are not really needed to perform a free throw, but these symptoms are very common in athletes we have worked with who are required to execute skills under pressure. Here is a more comprehensive idea of what many athletes tell us they experience prior to pressured skill execution:

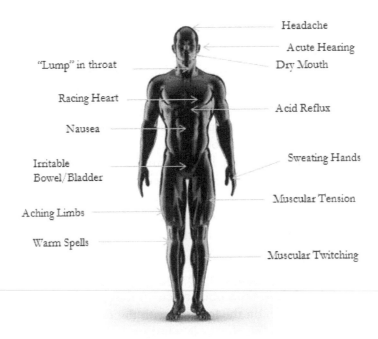

Headache

Acute Hearing

Dry Mouth

"Lump" in throat

Racing Heart

Nausea

Acid Reflux

Irritable
Bowel/Bladder

Sweating Hands

Muscular Tension

Aching Limbs

Warm Spells

Muscular Twitching

Evading the Sabre Toothed Tiger

Why do we experience these unnecessary symptoms? Basically, we are still playing catch up with civilisation. We have an inbuilt instinctual tendency to approach demanding situations like competitions as an existential matter of life or death. The body prepares itself physiologically as if it were about to engage in *fight or flight* behaviour, even though what is actually required is just to produce intricate skills.

But don't blame the body for this reaction. It's been programmed into us through millions of years of evolution. These reactions are one of the reasons we have survived, and thrived, as a species. In a fascinating book about emotions called "Should I Strap a Battery to my Head?" Gaurav Suri and Dr. James Gross of Stanford University put it like this:

"Imagine one of our early ancestors hearing a rattlesnake's rattle in close proximity to him. Right away, his hearing becomes more acute, and his peripheral

216

vision improves dramatically. He is able to detect sounds and motions that were previously imperceptible. At the same time, blood leaves his digestive tract and goes to his legs. His heart rate spikes. He is suddenly able to run faster than usual (if he decides to). He sees things around him through new eyes. A previously unnoticed branch now represents a potential weapon. His goals and priorities shift. A deer around the bend – usually an attractive prey for him – is able to walk by unnoticed. Memory systems are activated, bringing to mind what he has learned about avoiding sudden movements around snakes. Slowly he takes a step backward away from the snake, then another and another, eventually, at a safe distance, pausing to resume his previously interrupted activities." [8]

In the above narrative, a series of psychological and physiological reactions are triggered at precise moments to increase the likelihood (not a guarantee) of our early ancestor's survival. On surviving this traumatic episode, the early ancestor could then pass on the genes that enabled him to survive this endeavour to his offspring, thus instilling his instinct in future generations. Emotions were developed because they were, and remain, useful.

Fast-forward to the present, and these coordinated psychological and physiological reactions are not always an appropriate response. Because we sense danger in a final, or any competition, attention is naturally directed to potentially harmful cues in the environment, such as the opponent, the coach that always gives us a hard time, the supporters expecting you to succeed. You see, in our evolutionary past, the majority of life's demands were life-threatening, such as evading predators and securing food by hunting and killing other animals. But in modern times, the demands are mostly psychological, such as the danger of harm to our social status, or the danger of being rejected or disapproved of. Our bodies, however, react as if the dangers are life-threatening, hence the fight or flight reactions.

Our bodies are still playing catch-up to rapidly developing civilisation. We react to psychological demands like we react to physical danger.

217

But you can get ahead of the game. You can train the body to adapt to these dangers and react more appropriately. Throughout this book we have outlined skills and techniques that will help you harness your reactions to pressure situations. Indeed, it is important to remember our words from chapter 8 that physiological reactions can be highly beneficial if harnessed correctly, delivering blood to the brain so that you can make accurate and rapid decisions under pressure. But this chapter is about learning to thrive when it matters most by doing the very thing that you often want to most avoid... performing under pressure!

Choose Pressure

'Adapt' is about learning how to prepare for big competitions by choosing to face pressure regularly and by putting yourself in uncomfortable situations. More importantly, it is about *staying in there*. Indeed, much of elite sport performance is about learning to embrace and enjoy difficult situations. It makes sense that athletes who achieve World Records or win Olympic Gold medals are motivated by, and have a positive approach towards, the most pressured situations that they will ever encounter. If they felt threatened in any way about what they were going to do - it is more than likely they would render themselves too worried to realise their potential and may severely underperform. Chapter 9 is also about helping coaches and leaders to systematically and safely expose their athletes to pressure in order to desensitize them to the demands of performing in the high-pressure cooker that is elite sport.

Learn to embrace pressure. See it as a challenge, an opportunity to express yourself and demonstrate your capabilities.

First we start with how you, as an athlete, can develop your personal adaptation skills. There are four principles that can be practically applied:

1. Seek pressure
2. Create pressure
3. Stay in there
4. Phone a friend

1. Seek Pressure

I've never known anybody to achieve anything without overcoming adversity.[9]

Lou Holtz, American football player and coach, and active sports caster

You simply cannot *adapt* to adverse situations unless you actually *face* adverse situations.

Successful athletes seek new challenges and venture into adversity and pressure. It is not because they are successful that they so willingly crusade into unknown territory, it is because they crusade that they are successful.

Sure, you can bump along finding lots of creative ways to avoid stressful and pressured encounters, but it is those athletes who seek pressure who adapt more effectively. As a consequence they are able to deliver when it really counts.

Chapter 9

Desensitization

As touched upon in chapter 6, *desensitization* is a process of repeated exposure to adversity with the view of reducing emotional responses to it. So what was once a highly anxiety-provoking final becomes an exciting opportunity, for example.

Desensitization was pioneered by Mary Cover Jones (20th century American psychologist) and later Joseph Wolpe (South African psychiatrist, considered one of the most influential figures in behaviour therapy), who developed the idea of hierarchical or systematic desensitization.

Under Wolpe's methodology, an athlete develops a hierarchical list of feared stimuli ranked in order of least disturbing to the most disturbing. Then the athlete learns deep relaxation techniques (see Progressive Muscular Relaxation in chapter 8). Next, systematic desensitization begins. This involves the athlete gradually approaching ever increasing feared situations while staying relaxed. This works best when the athlete actually faces their feared situations, instead of merely imaging them. Ideally, this would be by performing in real life situations. Then the athlete slowly moves up the hierarchy until the last, and most feared, item on the list is performed without fear or anxiety.

A great example of desensitization was seen in a U.K. TV special called "Vertigo Road Trip". On the show, five people with a fear of heights were exposed to their worst nightmare: really high landmarks! Dr. Jennifer Wild of Oxford University led the group as they took on higher and higher landmarks: from a staircase in a London office to the Burj Khalifa in Dubai, which stands at 828m tall. Fascinatingly, as the five ventured into these feared endeavours, they began to acclimatize and overcome their fears.[10] Starting as jittery and panicky sceptics, the process transformed the participants into confident and rational individuals.

So, first things first. Have a go at developing your pressure hierarchy. This can include any situation in your sport in which you feel anxiety or stress. Remember, the situations should get more intense with anxiety as you go up the hierarchy. It may help to give each situation a severity rating between 0 and 100 - the higher the score the more severe the anxiety. This could include one specific situation in which multiple aspects cause anxiety. For example, when approaching the first round of a tournament maybe anxiety is experienced the night before when preparing kit, in the morning when you wake up to travel to the venue, when you are in changing rooms waiting to go onto the field of play, and when you walk out to perform. Or it could include lots of different situations in which you feel anxious. For example, tight matches, penalty situations, free kicks/throws, knock-out games, play-off matches.

My Pressure Hierarchy

Rank	Situation	Anxiety Rating (0-100)
1		
2		
3		
4		
5		
6		
7		
8		
9		
10		

Once you have created your hierarchy, revisit chapter 8 and really practice the relaxation strategies outlined. To get to the point where you are able to carry out your chosen relaxation technique in a real sport situation, try to memorise the process and get accustomed to feelings of self-induced relaxation.

The next step is encapsulated in the title of this section... Seek Pressure. This can be very difficult to do, but start at the bottom of your list and face each situation in turn. If we take tight or closely contested tennis matches, as an example, this may involve setting up training drills where you are just one point ahead or are drawing. It may involve imposing strict rules in these practice situations where forfeits are completed for poor performance, and rewards are earned for good performance. You may decide to take on tougher opponents in your pre-season warm-up. All of these activities provide you with real situations in which performance anxiety will be salient and therefore gives you a chance to work upwards on your hierarchy. It goes without saying - you have to be very committed to this process in order to make it work. But the benefits are priceless.

Research shows that repeated exposure to stressful activities can help people to adapt to stressful situations more easily, thus becoming better prepared for actual performance. People acclimatize to the experience of stress and anxiety and develop or learn personal and often implicit (subconscious) resources for performing under pressured conditions. Can you imagine facing all of your performance fears and conquering them? The amount of self-confidence gleaned from this experience is powerful, and it is little wonder that systematic desensitization boasts high rates of success for curing more serious anxiety-related issues (such as depression).[11]

So seek pressure, follow your list, and importantly reflect on your positive experiences to add to you visualization ammunition (see chapter 5).

2. Create Pressure

Let's be frank. You cannot, and nor should you, recreate 100% of the pressure of genuine competitions. This would be impossible and

223

actually a massive waste of time and effort. You cannot fool yourself into believing that a bogus 'pressure' situation is the real thing.

However, as it turns out, it is not necessary to create a situation that exactly matches a real pressure situation. Good evidence indicates that being exposed to a moderate amount of stress can help prevent you from succumbing to the real pressure of that all-important sport performance.

Professor Sian Beilock, expert in the breakdown of skilled performance under pressure, led a study that showed that golfers who practiced under pressure (by having their performance video-recorded), performed better in a subsequent pressure test than golfers who practiced in the absence of the video-recording. So, by training under pressured circumstances, the golfers were helped to cope with the pressure of actual competitive circumstances.[12]

Further, Associate Professor Mark Seery of the University of California looked at what factors increase the human ability to adapt to stressful situations. He pointed out how exposure to moderate levels of adversity - throughout life - helps people to view stress as a challenge whereas those exposed to very high levels, or very low levels saw stress in more threatening terms (see chapter 2 for the benefits of 'challenge'). In other words, exposure to some stress can be beneficial, and you can control this by creating pressure situations that speed up your adaptation.[13]

So, creating training environments that are intense and highly evaluative can help you to adapt to pressure and adversity. Research shows that individuals who perform well-learned tasks in front of an audience generate challenge states. This is because they have *knowledge of their abilities*, even though the audience was a significant stressor. In contrast, individuals who perform an unlearned task in front of an audience generate threat states. Because these individuals had no tried and tested skills, the stress of having an audience was too much to cope with.[14]

So, *practicing under pressure* is crucial for competing under pressure. The practice enables you to build confidence in the knowledge that you have the skills to perform well, and that you are able to cope with the pressure. In fact, research shows that as situations become *more* familiar, individuals react in a greater challenge state, rather than a threat state, due to enhanced coping perceptions.[15]

So how can you practically create pressure for yourself? Here are three strategies that we advocate to athletes in order to help them practice under pressure:

1. Mock competition: The idea of a mock probably brings back memories from school where you sat a mock exam in preparation for the real thing. Well, psychologically, this is incredibly important. Think of it as a dress rehearsal prior to opening night. The key here is to make the mock competition as realistic as possible, while acknowledging that it will not match the pressure of the real thing. It is important, with mock activities, to include critical peers that can take the place of spectators, scouts, or sponsors. It is also important that those peers play the part and be objective. Ask them to rate your performance and make notes about what you do wrong. Prepare as you would for the real thing and build in some time after the mock for feedback from your peers and some self-reflection. The point is that the mock aligns with your fears of judgment and negative evaluation.

2. Video record yourself and view it with your coach. Many athletes tell us that reviewing performance and training footage with the coach is actually more stressful than competing in front of strangers. Your coach knows you well and has certain expectations, and the danger that they will judge and then reject you is often more significant than the danger of being judged and rejected by strangers. You can use this to induce stress by video recording yourself training or (even better) in competition, and then sitting with your coach to review it. This may already be a part of your training – if so, great! – if it is not currently part of what you do then consider building it into your time with the coach. By facing up to the views of your coach, you can learn to face up to the views of strangers.

3. Practice worst-case scenarios: You are in the first round of a tournament and have been drawn to play against a player ranked 50 places below you. You are the favourite here. However, you go a set down and are a break down in the

second set. What do you do? Panic? Not if you have practiced this circumstance. Have your coach set up drills that put you in these tough circumstances, and add some jeopardy – a forfeit for failure – nothing too severe but something that will signal to you that you have not achieved. Rehearse worst-case scenarios so that you are you prepared for the possibility that your opponent plays the game of his or her career against you. Then in the event that the worst does occur, you can be confident in your ability to adapt.

The cliché is "fail to prepare and prepare to fail" but what we suggest is a lot more solution-focused than general preparation. Here, you target what you would consider to be the *worst thing* that could happen in an important situation. Michael Phelps, the most decorated Olympian of all-time, colours his goggles in with a black Sharpie, effectively making himself blind for when he needs to turn whilst in training in the pool. "It's weird, but we want to be ready for literally anything that comes our way. I never want to leave that comfort zone," Phelps explained. In Beijing, at the 2010 Olympics, when his goggles began to fill up with water during the 200m butterfly final, he was ready for it. "If I didn't prepare for everything that happens, when my goggles started filling up I'd have probably flipped out. That's why I swim in the dark."[16]

Imagine how stressful this must have been the first time Phelps did it in training. But not so stressful the second time, and even less stressful the third time. So practice coming back from unexpected set-backs. It may be frustrating to begin a training drill on a loss, but by practicing under these circumstances you are adapting; if a negative circumstance happens, you can remain composed and execute a different game plan to the one you arrived at the match with. Remember, preparation is a key source of self-confidence. So too is past performance success. Develop your skills at effectively performing under worst-case conditions.

Practice under pressure. Create pressure to give yourself the best opportunity for success.

Another way to create pressure, that is simple and easy to arrange, is to make yourself *accountable to yourself*. This involves rating 'yourself against yourself' with regards to a performance, for example. You may ask yourself the question: "If 100% represents me at my best, based on today's performance, what percentage do I give myself?" Be brutally honest here, there is no one to check on your scores.

An additional idea is to have the coaches, or the sport science team, do the same. Ask them the question: "If 100% represents me at my best, based on today's performance, what percentage do you give me?" When we use this with elite athletes we see a couple of interesting outcomes. The first is that you typically rate yourself lower than your coaches rate you, which may reflect a lack of confidence in a particular task (in which case read chapter 5 in this book). The second is that you rate yourself higher than your coaches rated you. This could reflect a lack of self-awareness on your part regarding your performance and the expectations of your coaches. So in your next performance your aim is to reduce this discrepancy so that your performance meets the required standards.

The creation of pressure is about performing under moderate stress and adversity, not about creatively inventing the most pressured situations you can imagine. Done right, you can learn to adapt to pressure and enjoy the developmental experiences of honing your performances through stressful and meaningful training situations.

3. Stay In There

Both seeking and creating pressure is of no use if, when faced with that pressure, you shy away or withdraw from it. While desensitization is a highly lauded and effective technique for overcoming fears and promoting adaptation, there is another more powerful method... but it's not for the faint-hearted.

'*Stay in there*' (also called '*flooding*') was developed by cognitive behavioural therapists to help people conquer their fears and it does exactly what it says on the can. When faced with adverse and pressured situations, remain in that situation until a) you feel comfortable, or b) it's over. This is tough because you are overriding your impulse to withdraw when you sense danger.

It takes a lot of willpower and determination, but the gains can surpass those gleaned from using desensitization alone. Desensitization allows you to be in control of your exposure to that which you fear. You try a little pressure, you withdraw, you try a little more pressure, you withdraw. But 'stay in there' requires you to try significant pressure straight off-the-bat and you do not withdraw until you get over your fear or the event is over. For clarity the key differences between desensitization and 'stay in there' are illustrated in the next diagram.

Both methods involve a level of discomfort, but 'stay in there' mimics actual sport performance more closely, in that it recreates what is really required of you in actual pressure situations. With real competitions, you cannot just walk away when the going gets tough or when you feel uncomfortable (or you can, but this is not the mark of an elite athlete).

'Staying in there' involves remaining in a difficult or pressured situation for as long as you can. Over time you learn to adapt.

You may have recognized by now that 'stay in there' is linked to Smart Thinking (see chapter 3) by creating evidence that adversity, no matter how severe, will not kill you, nothing 'terrible' will happen, and even if you don't perform so well - it will not be the end of the world.[17] In fact, rather than harming you, staying in there can help you develop your coping skills for stressful encounters.[18] Put another way, by forcing yourself, against your urges, to stay in there - you will adapt. There is a great story about how Joseph Wolpe (the South African psychiatrist we talked about earlier) helped a girl with a fear of cars to overcome this fear by driving her around in a car for four hours. At first the girl was hysterical, but she learned to cope with this fear and calm down when she realized the situation was safe. She got over her fear of cars by ironically and paradoxically being in a car until she felt okay.

So regardless of whether you choose to seek pressure or create pressure to develop your ability to adapt, 'staying in there' is a hugely powerful philosophy to have when approaching adverse conditions.

4. Phone a Friend

"Behind every great man there is a great woman" is a phrase which has been proffered many times in the public domain.[19] But from pressure and adaptation perspectives what does it actually imply beyond its literal meaning? From our experience what we note is that successful people have very strong and powerful support networks. This doesn't have to be a wife or partner, but can be other family, friends, colleagues, teammates, or support staff. These networks provide athletes with a foundation that they can use when situations are tough or when tough decisions need to be made.

Whilst Sir Alex Ferguson had one of the most successful managerial careers of all time with Manchester United Football Club, one of the consistent aspects, which he repeatedly discussed, was the support of his wife Cathy, his family, his close network of friends, and a comfortable home environment that allowed him respite and comfort. This all makes sense but - wait a minute - what we also observe in elite athletes is that the more successful they become the more they move beyond what they know and love; they often *lose their social support*.

When social support is lost, dealing with success and failure becomes problematic: making decisions becomes stressful, knowing who to trust is a challenge, and life becomes a struggle. We know from the vast amount of research regarding the psychology of injury that one of the key predictors of adherence to rehabilitation programmes and a successful return to competition is a solid social support network. Intuitively this makes sense; injury is painful, rehab even more so, hence having others to share concerns, give guidance, provide positive encouragement, and offer a shoulder to cry on, should never be overlooked. Overall, our advice to all athletes is to make sure they have the right people around them and to be aware of *why* they consider those people to be the right kind of people. For example, as an athlete you often require technical instruction, emotional support, and esteem support. The very best athletes are excellent at having a core number of people who can provide these needs when called upon.

Being a triathlete can be really self-absorbing. You have to make so many sacrifices - missing friends' weddings, staying behind on family trips. Getting together after a race is how I reconnect with the people who are important to me. I have to build that into my life - otherwise it's easy to let it slide. After being so focused on a race, it's nice to sit back and enjoy simple pleasures like a good laugh with the family.[20]

Laura Bennett, Triathlete

Scientifically we know that social support is a great stress buffer and can lead to substantial mental and physical health benefits over time.[21] That is, knowing that you have people you can turn to when things go awry, or that you have the support of your friends and family in the decisions you make, can relieve and even prevent stress and other psychological issues.

Recently scientific research has uncovered the amazing effects of a hormone called oxytocin. Oxytocin is released by the brain in response to stressful situations. But it also prompts a desire for social contact. Oxytocin released during positive (supportive) social contact - even if this social contact is anticipated - actually reduces the severity of the body's stress response. In fact a recent piece of research by Dr. Laura Kubzansky and colleagues at the Harvard School of Public Health has shown that when people are put under social stress (e.g., public speaking), oxytocin is associated with a challenge state and a healthier recovery profile after the stress.[22] In a nutshell, when facing a stressful situation, oxytocin can help you to deal better with stress. There is a fascinating and brilliantly presented TED talk by Dr. Kelly McGonigal on the subject, available online, if you are interested in finding out more.[23]

Social support is very important for dealing with stress.
Be aware of those who support your needs.

So, maintaining a strong and meaningful social support network is crucial. Not only does it provide instrumental support such as advice and guidance, but it also buffers stress and can even aid the production of helpful stress responses. The great four-time Olympic gold medal track and field athlete Jesse Owens said that, "Friendships born on the field of athletic strife are the real gold of competition. Awards become corroded, friends gather no dust."[24]

For Coaches

As a coach, you are partly responsible for how your athletes react in pressured and adverse situations. We want coaches and athletes to enjoy pressure, not be fazed by it (seeing it as integral part of elite performance and success).

Sir Alex Ferguson often spoke about wanting his Manchester United players to *enjoy the ball under pressure* and to *express themselves* - almost a rallying cry for them to show off their skills to the millions of spectators. Think for a moment how liberating such instruction from a leader would be. There is no mention of failure, making mistakes, or letting others down. Moreover, it creates an atmosphere of trust, autonomy, and competence.

You can provide verbal encouragement, lend an empathetic ear, and help to relax your athletes prior to their crucial competitions. However, there are more powerful developmental strategies that you can put in place to encourage adaptation in your team. Using the ideas we have discussed in this chapter, you can ensure that your athletes are regularly and safely exposed to moderate levels of pressure using isolated activities, or slight changes in the training environment. Here we advocate three activities that encapsulate what you have read in this chapter so far but which are reliant on you as a leader to implement. Make time for them with your team.

1. Personal-Disclosure Mutual-Sharing

2. Pressure Testing

3. Improvement Comparisons

1. Personal-Disclosure Mutual-Sharing

One activity that can help to desensitize athletes to the pressure of judgement and scrutiny, along with creating group beliefs and positive attitudes towards pressure, is Personal-Disclosure Mutual-Sharing (PDMS).[25]

PDMS requires athletes to publicly disclose previously unknown personal stories and information to the rest of their team.[26]

Stemming from counselling psychology, Personal-Disclosure symbolizes conscious verbal presentations of a situation or issue in an attempt to establish resolution through interpersonal interaction. Collaborative Personal-Disclosure underpinned by Mutual-Sharing can encourage empathetic responses between team members and foster enhanced understanding and an appreciation of one another's past and present experiences. PDMS provides the catalyst for the shared communication of morals, beliefs, attitudes, and personal motives, which in turn augment perceptions, meanings, constructs, and understanding.

Typically, in our work with elite athletes we encourage coaches to provide athletes with a series of questions or instructions that they are to prepare responses for, and then present to fellow team members, during a specifically arranged session. Indeed, the outcomes of PDMS are very much dependent on what is discussed during the sessions.

By encouraging disclosure of information about times of success, or how to deal with pressure, team members develop greater self-awareness and understanding of others. We have used PDMS with various teams across elite sport and have witnessed the powerful effect of sessions on the dynamic of the team and the thoughts and behaviours of the athletes involved. PDMS has the potential to help create a culture that embraces pressure and that deals with adversity effectively.

To illustrate, we applied PDMS in professional soccer where the needs presented by the coaches of the soccer team were for an intervention to foster team spirit.[27]

The club had reached the latter stages of a domestic cup competition and team functioning issues were emerging according to the manager, coaches, and senior players. The foreign players tended to socialize together and not with the rest of the team due to language and cultural differences. Players reported concerns regarding selection and playing time, and there was evidence of potential conflict between senior players and new additions to the squad.

With the aim of enabling the players to understand the motives and backgrounds of their teammates, an intervention that centred on the mutual sharing of personal information was proposed. Players were briefed, in advance, that the PDMS session would involve them sharing a personal story with their team-mates. Story content would centre around two guiding questions designed to raise team awareness of individual player identity, their motivation, and role perceptions. First, why they play soccer and what they bring to the team. Secondly, to describe a personal story that would help team-mates understand them better, that they would want the team to know, and that illustrates something that defined who they are.

Players were encouraged to speak honestly and openly about personal sacrifices that they had made in the pursuit of their soccer career. Support was given from the manager/coach to deliver the PDMS session in the team hotel prior to the important domestic cup semi-final game.

The session lasted for 90-minutes, and each player spoke for approximately three minutes. Players listened attentively to each of their teammates and spontaneously applauded each speech. Immediate responses to the session included one player saying that he 'wanted to hug' his teammates after hearing their stories and another who commented that if the player who had shared a particularly emotional story had cried - the whole team would have been in tears. The team performed above expectations in the semi-final, narrowly losing to the cup favourites in a penalty shoot-out. The PDMS session benefited the team: enhancing closeness, understanding of teammates, and communication.

There are instructions, in the book's appendix (Appendix 2), for any coach, or indeed captain, wishing to implement a PDMS session.

2. Pressure Testing

As we have outlined previously, desensitization to pressure is important to enable athletes to adapt, and one associated strategy we use is 'Pressure Testing'.

Pressure testing involves creating 'test' situations which mirror pressure situations in sport.[28, 29] For example, in our work with professional cricketers we structure pressure testing opportunities on key cricket skills into their training schedules (e.g., batting, bowling, and fielding).

For example, in our batting test we inform players that they are required to chase 36 runs from 30 deliveries against a pace bowling machine. In addition, they are informed that they are in competition with each other and that their scores will be posted for all to see (*ego threatening instructions*).

In soccer, we get athletes to face pressure scenarios. The athletes are told that they are 2-1 down and have 10 minutes left on the clock in which to get the game level in a hypothetical cup final. This kind of exercise can be tailored to specific pressured situations in which the athletes may have floundered in the past. For example, perhaps the drill is to face a free kick at the edge of the box in the last minute of the game, or perhaps the team need to score two goals in order to qualify for 'the next round' on goal difference.

The same principles can be applied in golf too. To illustrate, golfers may practice their putting by setting targets related to their distance from the hole. For four-foot putts a 100% success rate across a block of 20 putts may be set. If a putt is missed the golfer goes back to zero and they start again. Only when the threshold of 100% has been reached do they move onto a new distance where a new threshold or target is set (e.g., from 15-feet a success rate of 60% or 12 consecutive putts). This type of approach is something that most professional golfers adopt in their practice and pre-competition routine to prepare for the challenges of tournament play.

A perfect example (that is thankfully growing in popularity) of pressure testing is illustrated by Head Men and Women's Fencing Coach at Columbia University, Michael Aufrichtig. Mr. Aufrichtig helped his fencers to thrive in clutch situations (where the next point would win/lose the bout) by holding sudden-death drills. Teammates would face each other in training for a single point – the one-touch drill. If the fencer loses the point, they must perform a set of push-ups or lunges, or he/she can challenge his/her opponent to a double-or-nothing match. Mr. Aufrichtig describes fencing as "a mental game… people call it chess at 100 miles an hour." By training his athletes under pressure for these very specific pressure tests, when actual matches went to sudden death, his athletes prevailed. One fencer remarked "The one-touch drill is one of the reasons we're ranked No. 1 in the country."[30]

The premise of these tests is to regularly expose players to pressure so that they become desensitized (i.e., used to pressure) and are thus more able to deal with adversity during games. This premise is very much influenced by what we know from other disciplines including the military. Ultimately, these situations are created to reduce the likelihood of individuals choking under pressure when they eventually go into real life demanding situations.

From a coach's perspective it's about exposing athletes to pressure so that they learn to cope under such circumstances. From an athlete's, perceptive it's about seeking and creating pressure for themselves. What we find is that the more stressful tasks athletes complete, the more confident and composed they are about subsequent tasks. Once they recognize that they can cope, athletes can then start to work on thriving under pressure by developing their resources as covered in chapters 5, 6, and 7 in this book.

Pressure testing involves practicing under moderate-to-high pressure. Practice as you perform!

So pressure testing is a method to expose athletes to stress in controlled environments, helping them to adapt to these circumstances so that when a real pressure situation is met, it is approached with the confidence and composure we would expect from elite performers.

3. Improvement Comparisons

One of the many questions we get asked by coaches and athletes is how to recreate pressure outside of actual performance settings? This is indeed a good question and one that many England soccer coaches have juggled with when it comes to practicing penalties.

Former Blackburn Rovers soccer striker Jason Roberts, who was part of the BBC's presenting team for the 2014 Soccer World Cup, suggests that "It's one of those things I guess when people talk about preparing and taking penalties; it's about the pressure of that moment. You can't recreate the pressure of it especially in a World Cup. How do you replicate that?"[31] Roy Hodgson, England Team Head Coach, also recognizes that "you cannot recreate tired legs and the pressure, the feeling of great tension when they stand up to take a penalty."[32]

One of the mistakes, when it comes to designing pressure scenarios, is placing too great an emphasis on comparing individuals based purely on a performance score. Instead, coaches should work on developing individual targets for people that are not based on *overall levels of achievement* but based on *personal improvements*. In other words, make people accountable to themselves. Compare individuals to others based on how much they have improved, or indeed declined.

One mechanism to assist with this is through the public posting of league tables (in the training facility) regarding individual *improvement*. This mechanism ultimately adds an 'ego threat' (i.e., pressure) for athletes because nobody wants to demonstrate the least improvement by appearing at the bottom of the table.

In contrast, such a league table will almost certainly mobilise athletes' efforts to improve their performance say, for example, on fitness targets. *Mobilisation of effort* is one of the key benefits of using ego threat or competition scenarios. In essence, appropriate suggestions/situations are perceived as being meaningful by athletes and, hence, they become activated to do their best.

One real-world example from sport is to make fitness test results public. When we say public, we mean visible to all members of the team, not the general public. But importantly, it is not the actual results that are displayed, but the changes in scores from the last round of fitness tests. The fact that all scores will be seen adds some competitive pressure to the training environment to ensure that athletes put their all into training as well as in actual matches. It is constant improvement that professional organizations are interested in; this method helps to instil this philosophy in athletes.

It is important to standardize the way pressure is induced in athletes. We need to be sure that everyone is getting the same information and that their reactions are due to the information provided, not the way the information is delivered. In the appendix (Appendix 3) there are some instructions that we used to create increased pressure in a study that involved elite footballers and performance on a soccer skills task.[33]

From a coach's perspective consider the language that is used and how you could adapt these types of instructions to formulate improvement comparisons within the team. It is good practice to set up pressure tests and this is one way you can make a situation stressful so that your athletes can experience performing when the going gets tough.

Brief Summary

In this chapter we have introduced you to the notion that one of the greatest tools you have in your arsenal for performance is the ability to adapt to tough situations.

By developing this ability, and exploiting it, you can learn to thrive under pressure and deliver performances in the toughest of sport situations. This learning process is your responsibility. If you are a leader (coach, manager, captain), then you have a responsibility to help those around you to make the most of their propensity to adapt.

Most Important Point

Learning to adapt to pressure and adversity involves facing pressure, but also having the right support in place. As Frank Herbert says in the poem that starts this chapter, "I will face my fear."

Face *your* fear.

[1] Youngs, I. (2002, December 21). 50 Cent: The $1m rapper. *BBC News*. Retrieved May 21, 2014, from http://news.bbc.co.uk/1/hi/entertainment/music/2591521.stm

[2] 50 Cent net worth. (n. d.). In *celebritynetworth.com*. Retrieved May 21, 2014, from http://www.celebritynetworth.com/richest-celebrities/richest-rappers/50-cent-net-worth/

[3] Morrison, M. (2007). Muhammad Ali Timeline. *In infoplease.com*. Retrieved May 21, 2014, from http://www.infoplease.com/spot/malitimeline1.html

[4] Muhammad Ali (n. d.). *In brainyquote.com*. Retrieved May 21, 2014, from http://www.brainyquote.com/quotes/authors/m/muhammad_ali.html

[5] Worthy, D. A., Markman, A. B., & Maddox, W. T. (2009). Choking and excelling at the free throw line. *The International Journal of Creativity & Problem Solving, 19*, (1), 53-58.

[6] Baumeister, R. F., & Steinhilber, A. (1984). Paradoxical effects of supportive audiences on performance under pressure: The home field disadvantage in sports championships. *Journal of Personality and Social Psychology, 47*, (1), 85-93.

[7] Goldman, M., & Rao, J. M. (2012). Effort vs. concentration: The asymmetric impact of pressure on NBA performance. *MIT Sloan Sports Analysis Conference*, March 4-5.

[8] Suri, G., & Gross, J. J. (2012). What good are emotions anyway? In P. Totterdell and K. Niven (Eds.). *Should I strap a battery to my head? (and other questions about emotion)*. Charleston, SC: Createspace Independent Publishing

[9] Success/Sports-Related Quotations (2002, December 1st). *In smiley963.tripod.com*. Retrieved May 21, 2014, from http://smiley963.tripod.com/sports.html

[10] Vertigo Roadtrip (2014, May 7). *The BBC*. Retrieved May 21, 2014, from http://www.bbc.co.uk/programmes/b0436rpk

[11] Wolpe, J. (1990). *The practice of behavior therapy (4th ed.)*. Oxford, England: Pergamon Press, Inc.

[12] Beilock, S.L., & Carr, T.H. (2001). On the fragility of skilled performance: What governs choking under pressure? *Journal of Experimental Psychology: General, 130*, 701–725.

[13] Seery, M. D. (2011). Challenge or threat? Cardiovascular indexes of resilience and vulnerability to potential stress in humans. *Neuroscience & Biobehavioral Reviews, 35*, 1603-1610 http://dx.doi.org/10.1016/j.neubiorev.2011.03.003.

[14] Blascovich, J., Mendes, W. B., Hunter, S. B., & Salomon, K. (1999). Social "facilitation" as challenge and threat. *Journal of Personality and Social Psychology, 76*, 68-77.

[15] Blascovich, J., Mendes, W. B., Hunter, S. B., & Salomon, K. (1999). Social "facilitation" as challenge and threat. *Journal of Personality and Social Psychology, 76*, 68-77.

[16] White, D. (2012, July 15). London 2012 Olympics: Michael Phelps sets mind's eye on triumphant role in final part of Lord of the Rings trilogy. *The Telegraph*. Retrieved May 21, 2014, from http://www.telegraph.co.uk/sport/olympics/swimming/9401518/London-2012-Olympics-Michael-Phelps-sets-minds-eye-on-triumphant-role-in-final-part-of-Lord-of-the-Rings-trilogy.html

[17] Ellis, A., & Dryden, W. (1997). *The practice of rational-emotive behavior therapy*. New York: Springer Publishing Company.

[18] Dobson, K. S. (2010). *Handbook of cognitive-behavioral therapies* (3rd ed.). New York, NY: The Guilford Press.

[19] The meaning and origin of the expression: Behind every great man there's a great woman (n. d.). In *phrases.org.uk* Retrieved May 21, 2014 http://www.phrases.org.uk/meanings/60500.html

[20] Pashman, H. (2012, July 16). Make Time for Family and Friends. *In shape.com*. Retrieved May 21, 2014, from http://www.shape.com/celebrities/interviews/inspirational-quotes-olympic-athletes/slide/7

[21] Cohen, S., & McKay, G. (1984). Social support, stress and the buffering hypothesis: A theoretical analysis. In A. Baum, S. E. Taylor, & J. E. Singer (Eds.), *Handbook of Psychology and Health*. Hillsdale, NJ: Laurence Erlbaum.

[22] Kubzansky, L. D., Mendes, W. B., Appleton, A.A., Block, J., & Adler, G.K. (2012). A heartfelt response: Oxytocin effects on response to social stress in men and women. *Biological Psychology. 90*, (1), 1-9. doi: 10.1016/j.biopsycho.2012.02.010

[23] McGonigal, K. (2013). My TED talk "how to make stress your friend". *TED*. Retrieved May 21, 2014, from

http://kellymcgonigal.com/2013/12/31/watch-my-ted-talk-how-to-make-stress-your-friend/

[24] Jesse Owens Biography (n. d.). *In biography.com*. Retrieved May 21, 2014, from http://www.biography.com/people/jesse-owens-9431142#synopsis

[25] Dunn, J. G. H., & Holt, N. L. (2004). A qualitative investigation of a personal-disclosure mutual-sharing team building activity. *The Sport Psychologist, 18*, 363-380.

[26] Evans, A., Slater, M. J., Turner, M. J., & Barker, J. B. (2013). Using Personal-Disclosure and Mutual-Sharing to enhance group functioning in a professional soccer academy. *The Sport Psychologist, 27*, (3), 233-243.

[27] Windsor, P. M., Barker, J., & McCarthy, P. (2011). Doing Sport Psychology: Personal-Disclosure Mutual-Sharing in Professional Soccer. *The Sport Psychologist, 25*, (1), 940 114.

[28] Turner, M. J., & Barker, J. B. (2013). Resilience: Lessons from the 2012 Olympic Games. *Reflective Practice, 14*, (5), 622-631.

[29] Turner, M. J., Jones, M. V., Sheffield, D., Slater, M. J., Barker, J. B., & Bell, J. (2013). Who thrives under pressure? Predicting the performance of elite academy cricketers using the cardiovascular indicators of challenge and threat states. *Journal of Sport and Exercise Psychology, 35*, (4), 387-397.

[30] Kilgannon, C. (2014, February 7). No. 1 Columbia Fencers Are Aided by 'Jedi Master'. *The New York Times*. Retrieved May 21, 2014, from http://www.nytimes.com/2014/02/08/nyregion/no-1-columbia-fencers-aided-by-a-jedi-master.html?_r=0

[31] Echo Reporter. (2014, May 7). BBC to broadcast guide on taking penalties to help England at world cup. *Evening Echo*. Retrieved May 21, 2014, from http://www.eveningecho.ie/2014/05/07/bbc-to-broadcast-guide-on-taking-penalties-to-help-england-at-world-cup/

[32] Pilditch, D. (2012, June 25). England's Euro 2012 dream ends after penalty shoot-out. *The Express*. Retrieved May 21, 2014, from http://www.express.co.uk/news/uk/328711/England-s-Euro-2012-dream-ends-after-penalty-shoot-out

[33] Barker, J. B., Jones, M. V., & Greenlees, I. (2010). Assessing the immediate and maintained effects of hypnosis on self-efficacy and soccer wall-volley performance. *Journal of Sport & Exercise Psychology, 32*, 243-252.

Chapter 10: Look Forward

Success is living up to your potential. That's all. Wake up with a smile and go after life... Live it, enjoy it, taste it, smell it, feel it.[1]

Joe Kapp, NFL Quarterback

Our main objective in this book was to take you on a psychological journey of self-discovery and self-improvement. We hope that we have met this objective.

The topics in this book introduce many skills and strategies that are supported by scientific research, have been used with elite athletes across a vast range of sports, and which are 'doable'. By doable we mean that the chapters offer simple and practical guidance, as well as justification for why and how the skills work.

The Future ain't what it used to be.[2]

Yogi Berra, Baseball Player

This book introduced you to The MAPP for Success with a view to helping you to influence each aspect of it, so that you can approach your sport performance in the best possible mental and physical state. Each step of The MAPP is linked with the next, and along the way there are key skills to develop and master in order to ensure that you fulfil your potential when it matters most.

The MAPP is a framework that you can refer to at any point. By critically engaging with The MAPP it is possible to recognize gaps in your performance mindset. That is, at each step we encourage you to honestly reflect on your performance approach and ask: "Am I doing everything I possibly can to maximize my potential?" and "What can I do better, to ensure peak performance when it matters most?"

Spot Check

Let's take a systematic approach to the endeavour of looking forward. It is important to understand *where you are* so you know *where you need to go*. Knowing that each step contributes to overall performance, the best way to get a spot check of where you are (on The MAPP) is to self-assess each step in turn. The beauty of this approach is that you can come back, time and time again, for a mindset check-up. Think of it as servicing your mindset, like you would your car.

Once you have identified areas of improvement, you can refer back to previous chapters for a refresher, to develop your skills further. In the present chapter we will move through The MAPP and talk about how you can use each element to aid your personal development and goal achievement. We begin with a reminder of The MAPP for Success.

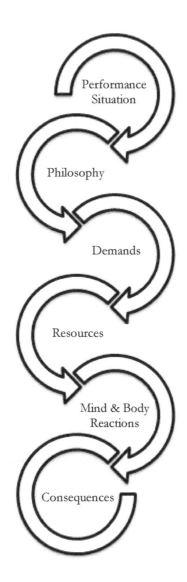

Performance Situation

Be specific. It is common for athletes to have different approaches to different performance situations. So our first piece of guidance here is to develop a MAPP for each of your most common performance situations. This is because each situation has different 'demand' characteristics. The demands of a cup final are different to a trial or fitness test. While all are important, each will have a different level of danger to esteem, requirement for effort, and uncertainty. In addition, the behaviours you wish to adopt will differ across situations. For example, in a cup final maybe it pays to be more pumped so that your performance is energetic and assertive, whereas in a fitness test it is composure that is more important. Maybe you want the coaching staff to see how unflustered you are by their testing during team meetings.

So, for each performance situation, you should have a different approach. The approaches are, of course, informed by The MAPP (as it is important in all performance situations to be highly confident, for example) and you need to be smart about the way you think about the situation. But the specific strategies you use to create confidence and Smart Thinking will be slightly different depending on the situation. Hence the creation of separate MAPPs for your most common performance situations (e.g., finals, trials, tests). The job is the same - to get into the right mindset - but the specific tools you use can differ across situations.

Don't approach every situation in exactly the same way. Of course, it makes perfect sense to approach different trials in a similar way (each time you attend a trial), as this can be a potent routine. But don't use your fitness test approach for a trial or final. Different events require different tools – you wouldn't use a saw to hammer a nail!

Have separate MAPPs for different performance situations.

Let's look at an example of how you can use the MAPP for a trial where a new contract is at stake. Each section in the flow diagram below has been completed with a few key phrases that reinforce each element of The MAPP, while evoking some of the skills we have discussed throughout the book.

Performance Situation

Competition in front of scouts

My Philosophy

I want the scouts to be impressed, but it's not the end of the world if they are not

Demands

I can't be sure of what the scouts will think, so I'd better put in 100% effort, as this is important for my career

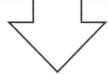

Resources

Real-time best-performance imagery has helped me to feel confident, I have done my pre-performance routine so I know I am ready, and I am completely focused on what I need to do to perform well

Mind & Body

My anxiety and nerves are here to help my body and mind perform under pressure

At each stage you can choose what strategy you will use to achieve your desired mental and physical state. Your philosophy about approaching a final will be different to a trial, so too will the demands, and therefore the strategies you choose to increase your resources (self-confidence, control, approach goals) will also differ. Your mind and body strategy may be to relax using focused breathing or to get energized using music, for example. In this book we have provided you with a number of resources for being creative in the way you approach any performance situation. Remember, the key principle is to *tip the balance*; ensure that you have specific strategies for enhancing and maintaining your resources in the face of pressure.

Philosophy

What are you telling yourself about a given situation that is leading to unhelpful feelings and behaviours? This is a key question when it comes to Smart Thinking introduced in chapter 3.

It is so important that you regularly assess the demands you place on yourself and the extent to which you use illogical and nonsensical thoughts in response to adversity. One of the best ways to gain an insight into your philosophy is to ask, "What am I telling myself about the situation that is causing me to feel anxious or angry or depressed?" Looking back to chapter 3, remember it is the B (the thoughts and beliefs) that cause your emotions and behaviours (C), not the situation itself (A).

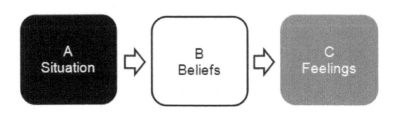

So complete the short questionnaire below, it is taken from an inventory we have developed to assess peoples' philosophies in performance settings.

About_____ (situation) I am telling myself...

		Totally Disagree				Totally Agree
1	I must not fail in things that are important to me	1	2	3	4	5
2	I must reach my goals	1	2	3	4	5
3	It's dreadful to not succeed in things that matter to me	1	2	3	4	5
4	It's terrible to fail in important tasks	1	2	3	4	5
5	I can't bear not succeeding in things that are important to me	1	2	3	4	5
6	I can't stand failing in important tasks	1	2	3	4	5
7	If I fail in things that matter to me, it means I am a failure	1	2	3	4	5
8	I am a loser if I do not succeed in things that matter to me	1	2	3	4	5

Questions 2, 3, 5, and 8 reflect your philosophy about achievement in the things that matter to you, whereas questions 1, 4, 6, and 7 reflect your philosophy about failure in the things that matter to you. If you score 3 and above for achievement and or failure (on average), then re-read chapter 3 and start to change these illogical demands to logical preferences. Remember, these illogical beliefs are unhelpful for emotions, behaviours, and ultimately performance.

Demands

Demands are what make important performance situations stressful. So, monitoring and being aware of demands is important so that you can understand what you are up against. Ignorance is no excuse when it comes to performing when it matters most, and you do not want to find yourself under-resourced because you did not grasp the demands of the situation.

Furthermore, you may find that by understanding the demands you realize that, actually, the situation isn't too bad at all and you actually require limited resources in order to succeed. Self and situational awareness are vital here.

Demands comprise three elements: uncertainty, requirement for effort, and danger to esteem. Uncertainty reflects the fact that, in sport performance, few outcomes are certain. Requirement for effort is about how much effort you need to exert in order to succeed (success usually does not come easily!), and danger to esteem is about the effects of success or failure on how you view yourself and how others view you. For example, a common thought is that if you fail, others will think less of you, or you will be embarrassed, or you will think less of yourself. These types of thoughts can damage your esteem. You can get a spot check on these demands after you have re-familiarized yourself with the resources.

Demands comprise uncertainty, requirement for effort, and danger to esteem.

Resources

Resources are, of course, the most important aspect of The MAPP as they dictate your responses to the important performance situation you are faced with. There are three resources: self-confidence, control, and achievement goals. In this book, there is a chapter for each resource to help develop highly potent and robust resources for all sorts of performance situations.

High resources are the key to success because they reflect well-documented and highly powerful psychological states that help to produce optimal sport performance. By developing the skills to enhance and maintain self-confidence, a focus on controllables, and a focus on success, you can tip the balance in your favour. Remember, tipping the balance means that your resources outweigh demands. By doing this you are likely to get into a challenge state (which has beneficial mind and body consequences) and fulfil your potential when it counts. A recap of the resources would perhaps be helpful here:

Self-Confidence: Belief in your ability to perform well in a given task.

Control: The extent to which performance is under your control.

Achievement Goals: Striving to achieve (good) or trying to avoid failure (bad).

A really neat way to get a spot check of your demands and resources is simply to graph your current levels of each element. Below you will see a graph with an ascending scale from 0 (very low) to 4 (very high). Across the bottom of the graph you will see each of the demands (on the left side) and each of the resources (on the right side). Your job (honesty is crucial) is to rate your current levels of demands and resources concerning the next important situation you will face in your sport.

Resources comprise self-confidence, control, and approach goals.

With regards to _____ (situation):

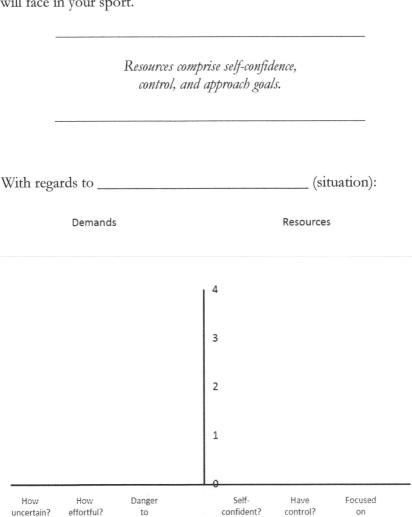

Demands				Resources		
How uncertain?	How effortful?	Danger to esteem?		Self-confident?	Have control?	Focused on Success?

Now take the average for the left side (scores for each of the three demands divided by 3), and the average for the right side (scores for each of the three resources divided by 3). You now have an indication of whether you have tipped the balance, and to what extent. If your demands score is higher than your resources score, you have not yet tipped the balance and should re-read chapters 5, 6, and 7, as they detail various evidence-based strategies that increase the resources. If your resources score is higher than your demands score, happy days! But don't get too cocky; make sure you maintain these high resources in the lead-up to your performance to make sure you are in a challenge state when it really counts.

Mind and Body Reactions

Chapters 2 through 7 deal with your thoughts and beliefs about the performance situation and yourself. But Chapters 8 and 9 are different because they are about regulating and adapting to how you feel prior to, and within, performance situations. Perhaps you want to feel relaxed prior to the competition, or maybe you prefer to feel pumped up and excited? Chapter 8 introduced tools that can help you get into your desired mental and physical state, whilst chapter 9 guided you through the steps that can help you to adapt to tough situations so that you feel ready when faced with pressure, instead of panicky.

Chapters 8 and 9 go hand-in-hand because to adapt you need to be able to self-regulate in actual performance situations. The tools we introduced in chapter 8 are great for any time of the day, but to use them in actual performance situations takes practice under pressure. Practice under pressure will help you adapt to pressure and strengthen your ability to self-regulate when the going gets tough… when it matters most.

Johnny Wilkinson (one of the world's best rugby union players) is a master of self-regulation under pressure, and he achieved this by being able to regulate his thoughts and feelings, and by facing countless pressure situations. He learned to self-regulate under pressure over *years* of performance and practice.

"People always tell you to shut it out, but I don't think you can. You don't close yourself off from the pressure. You just have to live with it, accept the fact it's there and function as normally as you would if it wasn't there. When everything is going crazy around you and the nerves are attacking your confidence, it's important to keep everything exactly the same."[3]

Here Wilkinson is talking about accepting the pressure and regulating himself under that pressure so that he can function normally (normal for him means highly skilled).

In training, Wilkinson placed great significance on increasing the pressure and making practice harder and harder. "For me it's very important to try and make it harder, more stress, more pressure, more difficult, all those things in training than it possibly could be in a game." He would take kicks and try to hit the rugby posts and crossbar from extreme angles, angles that he would not normally expect to face in a game. If he could handle the pressure here, then taking kicks from less extreme angles in a game would be less pressured. "Trying to hit that kick, professional pride means that the butterflies are flying around, and it's not a bad thing."

So, even in practice, Wilkinson felt the bodily effects of pressure because he had made training difficult and meaningful. "I'm stood there and I can actually see my shirt moving with the heartbeat. If you can get comfortable with being under pressure, being anxious and nervous, then it becomes second nature." This last point is crucial and is at the core of chapters 8 and 9. If you are able to adapt to pressure and stress by becoming comfortable, or becoming acclimatized to the feelings of stress, then you can function normally under that pressure.

Practicing under pressure will help you adapt to pressure and strengthen your ability to self-regulate when the going gets tough.

So use the biofeedback advice we gave you and regularly practice your ability to self-regulate in difficult situations.

Consequences

You don't run 26 miles at five minutes a mile on good looks and a secret recipe.[4]

**Frank Shorter,
Track Athlete**

You get out what you put in. There are no secrets to success in sport. It's about having all the right ingredients in your recipe that merge to form a winning mindset.

The consequences of using the techniques in this book will be that you are more likely to fulfil your potential. Successful athletes work hard at being successful, and this includes working hard to get their mindset right. Of course, using sport psychology to aid your performance is one part of what it takes to be successful. A sound mental approach will not turn you into a Tony Stark ("Ironman") overnight. But you are much more likely to achieve your goals with robust mental skills than without.

Luck? Sure. But only after long practice and only with the ability to think under pressure.[5]

**Babe Didrikson Zaharias,
All-Round Athlete**

Working hard at being successful is at the core of what chapter 10 is all about. The real lesson of this chapter is that your development doesn't end with this book. With continued effort and the strategic utilization of each chapter, you can keep building your resources, and keep refining your ability to react well to pressure and adversity. As a consequence, you will tip the balance in your favour when you perform in your sport.

Brief Summary

In this chapter, we have talked about how this book and its themes can be used, continuously, to help you get better at what you do, and more importantly, to help you fulfil your potential when it matters most.

This "fulfil your potential" idea has been flagged up a lot throughout this book, and some of you may be curious as to why we have opted for this turn of phrase instead of "ensure success" or "be victorious" under pressure. Well, *we* see it like this. The skills and strategies you take with you, and continue to develop, will help you to be the best 'you' when you need to be the best you when competing.

Be the best you when you need to be the best you.

In any sport performance situation we operate within our potential, and most of us operate at a level significantly below that potential. This book will help you to perform closer to that potential and *even reach it* if you are particularly dedicated to harnessing the power of your mind in performance situations.

We hope you have enjoyed your journey so far. Make unlocking your potential a continuous, enjoyable, and rewarding experience. Good luck and may you 'tip the balance' in all of your endeavours!

The will to win, the desire to succeed, the urge to reach your full potential... these are the keys that will unlock the door to personal excellence.[6]

Confucius, Chinese teacher, politician, and philosopher

[1] Inspirational sports quotes for all (n. d.). *In motivationalstory.com.* Retrieved May 21, 2014, from http://www.motivational-story.com/inspirational-sports-quotes.html

[2] Yogi Bera. (n. d.). *In wkikquote.org.* Retrieved May 21, 2014, from http://en.wikiquote.org/wiki/Yogi_Berra

[3] DigitalNewsAgency (2010, October 12). Jonny Wilkinson reveals his secrets for dealing with stress. *In youtube.com.* Retrieved May 21, 2014, from http://www.youtube.com/watch?v=0V5ZzXbWuq8

[4] Jarski, R. (2004). *The funniest thing you never said: The ultimate collection of humorous quotations.* London: Ebury Press.

[5] Babe Didrikson Zaharias (n. d.). *In athleticpoets.tumblr.com.* Retrieved May 21, 2014, from http://athleticpoetics.tumblr.com/post/38342744859/luck-sure-but-only-after-long-practice-and-only

[6] Confucius (2011, April 17). *In philosiblog.com.* Retrieved May 21, 2014, from http://philosiblog.com/2011/04/17/250/

Appendices

Appendix 1

Assessing My Response to Pressure

Box 1: Indicate how true the statements below are - regarding the upcoming important performance situation

		Not True At All					Totally True
1	I absolutely must perform well	1	2	3	4	5	6
2	If I fail, I am a failure	1	2	3	4	5	6
3	It would be terrible to fail	1	2	3	4	5	6
4	I couldn't stand/bear not succeeding	1	2	3	4	5	6

Scoring: Add each item score, then divide by four. This gives you a Smarter Thinking score.

My Smarter Thinking Score =

Box 2: Complete the following items in relation to the upcoming important performance situation

		Not At All					Extremely
1	How effortful (mental and or physical) do you expect the situation to be?	1	2	3	4	5	6
2	How uncertain is the outcome of the situation for you?	1	2	3	4	5	6

		Not True At All					Totally True
3	If I don't perform well, I will think less of myself.	1	2	3	4	5	6
4	If I don't perform well, others will think less of me.	1	2	3	4	5	6

Scoring: Add each item score, then divide by four. This gives you a Demands score.

My Demands Score =

Box 3: Complete the following items in relation to the upcoming important performance situation

		Not At All					Extremely
1	How confident are you in your ability to perform well in the situation?	1	2	3	4	5	6
2	How confident are you in your ability to cope in the situation?	1	2	3	4	5	6
3	How much do you feel your performance in the situation is under your personal control?	1	2	3	4	5	6
4	How much do you feel that the more effort you put in, the better you will perform?	1	2	3	4	5	6

		Not True At All					Totally True
5	It is important for me to perform as well as I possibly can	1	2	3	4	5	6
6	It is important for me to do well compared to others	1	2	3	4	5	6

Scoring: Add each item score. This gives you a Resources score.

My Resources Score =

Now for the harder maths...

Multiply your score for Box 1 (Smarter Thinking Score) with your score from Box 2 (Demands Score). Then take that result away from your score from Box 3 (Resources Score). You should arrive at a score somewhere between -30 and 35. This is your Challenge and Threat Score.

My Challenge and Threat Score =

The closer you are to 35, the more likely you are to approach the performance in a challenge state. The closer you are to -30, the more likely you are to approach the performance in a threat state. To improve your score, read chapters 5 to 7 to increase your resources.

Appendix 2

PDMS Instructions for Group Confidence

Dear Delegate,

As part of our ongoing development programme we require you to prepare and deliver a series of talks to a small group; therefore please respond to the questions below. It is important that you spend time thinking about your answers. Please come along to the session having prepared your talk. Please avoid putting on a performance. Just be open and honest with us.

1. How confident are you in your sport performance?
2. Where do you get your confidence from?
3. What aspects of your performance are you confident with?
4. What aspects of your performance do you lack confidence in?
5. How do you feel when you are confident?
6. How do you perform in your sport when you are confident?

PDMS Instructions for Pressure

Dear Delegate,

As part of our ongoing development programme we require you to prepare and deliver a series of talks to a small group; therefore please respond to the questions below. It is important you spend time thinking about your answers. Please come along to the session having prepared your talk. Please avoid putting on a performance. Just be open and honest with us.

1. How do I perform under pressure?
2. How does my body feel when under pressure?
3. What are my thoughts when under pressure?
4. What are my coping strategies when I am under pressure?

5. What pressure situations am I likely to experience in the forthcoming months?

It is important that coaches develop instructions that do not require individuals to disclose deeply personal information or any information which compromises fellow group members. Aligned with this it is also important to create a safe environment for individuals to enable them to feel comfortable in the content of their speeches and their possible emotional reactions. On all occasions we advocate a period of contracting at the start of each session to establish confidentiality and a code of conduct. This contracting comprises of open discussion and the collation of thoughts on flip-chart paper. Without this aspect, it is unlikely individuals will feel comfortable enough to deliver highly emotional information.

Appendix 3

Increased Pressure Instructions

When you come to perform the soccer wall volley task there will be substantial cash prizes available. What we are doing in this first performance is seeing how well you do in comparison to other participants involved in the study. Consequently, you will have to try very hard if you are to perform well in comparison to these other participants. All results will be distributed at the end of the phase and these will be publicly posted in ranking order for all participants to view.

Please remember that there are substantial cash prizes available for the best performers on the soccer volley task. Your score on this trial will count towards whether you win a cash prize or not. Therefore, you will have to perform well today to stand any chance of winning a cash prize. Your performance today will also be video recorded, then viewed and evaluated by a qualified football coach. From this evaluation you will be given a performance score. This score will form part of your overall performance score.

Index

Index

Index

Other Books From Bennion Kearny

The Successful Golfer: Practical Fixes for the Mental Game of Golf by Dr Paul McCarthy and Dr Marc Jones

The Successful Golfer is designed to help address 50 of the most common faults that players experience and which hold them back. These include: hitting the self-destruct button when winning, nervousness on the first tee, lost confidence, failing to 'practise as you play', and many more. Each fault is remedied with a clear practical fix. Readers will learn to develop effective practice plans, build a dependable pre-shot routine, and cope with the pressures of competitive golf. In the second part of the book, lessons from 30 fascinating research studies on golf are presented to help keep readers ahead of the field. They include research on putting, practice, choking, and overthinking. In the third and final part of the book, clear instructions are provided on developing a number of highly effective techniques that can be used across a wide variety of situations. These include: pre-shot routines, breathing exercises, goal setting, and how best to practice.

Golf Tough: Practice, Prepare, Perform and Progress by Dan Abrahams

Dan Abrahams is Lead Psychologist for England Golf, as well as a former touring professional golfer, and PGA coach. In Golf Tough, Dan offers you a powerful blueprint for improvement and a detailed plan for consistent high performance no matter what your standard of play. If you want to significantly lower your handicap, compete with greater consistency, win tournaments or reach the next level on the course, Dan's simple yet powerful philosophies, tools and techniques will help you break through your current barriers and reach your golfing goals.

The 7 Master Moves of Success by Jag Shoker

One of the most common clichés about success - that it is a journey, not a destination - has concealed one if its most defining qualities. Success really is a dynamic and ever-moving process. It is about making the right moves at the right time. In this absorbing and uplifting book, Jag Shoker – a leading performance coach to business leaders, sports professionals and creative performers – brings the science and inspiration behind success to life. He reveals the 7 Master Moves that combine to create the high performance state that he calls Inspired Movement: the ability to perform an optimal series of moves to create the success you desire most. Drawing widely on scientific research, his extensive consultancy experiences, and insights into the successes of top performers in business, sport, and entertainment, 7 Master Moves is a synthesis of the leading-edge thinking, and paradigms, that underpin personal performance and potential.

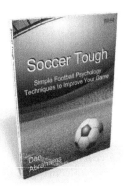

Soccer Tough: Simple Football Psychology Techniques to Improve Your Game by Dan Abrahams

Technique, speed and tactical execution are crucial components of winning soccer, but it is mental toughness that marks out the very best players – the ability to play when pressure is highest, the opposition is strongest, and fear is greatest. Top players and coaches understand the importance of sport psychology in soccer but how do you actually train your mind to become the best player you can be?

Soccer Tough demystifies this crucial side of the game and offers practical techniques that will enable soccer players of all abilities to actively develop focus, energy, and confidence. Soccer Tough will help banish the fear, mistakes, and mental limits that holds players back.

Coaching For The Zone: A Practitioner's Guide to Coaching for Business and Sport by Ted Garratt

Many people think The Zone is a matter of luck; it either happens or it doesn't. Because of this they don't plan for the Zone and when it happens don't know how to repeat it. In Coaching For The Zone leading coach practitioner and trainer Ted Garratt guides the reader through the process of training clients to enter The Zone. He demonstrates how to coach for The Zone to equip individuals with the skills and confidence to break through barriers and transform their abilities. The book is split into two sections. The first section follows an 8-part coaching programme with a coachee in a business environment, but also includes examples and case histories from sport. The second section contains Key Skills and Exercises that the practitioner can use when coaching clients for The Zone.

The Psychology of Cricket: Developing Mental Toughness by Dr. Stewart Cotterill and Dr. Jamie Barker

The mental side of cricket is what separates the best players from the rest. Technical, tactical, and physical preparation are important for top class performances but it is often what happens inside a player's mind that is the difference between success and failure. Whether batting, bowling, or fielding, a player's psychological strength has been identified by coaches, players, and commentators as a critical ingredient for winning cricket matches.

The Psychology of Cricket teaches individuals to develop mental toughness by using mental skills which can be used in both practice and match situations. The book also provides expert advice on understanding the important ingredients of successful teams and leaders.

Other Books From Bennion Kearny

Steel and Grace: Sheffield's Olympic Track and Field Medallists by Matthew Bell and Gary Armstrong

Steel and Grace examines the lives and careers of athletes who stood on the medal podium and positions their achievements within the political events that impacted upon the Games: in Berlin as Hitler showcased his Nazi regime; in Munich when terrorists murdered 11 Israeli athletes; in Moscow when British athletes competed against the wishes of the UK Government at the height of the Cold War.

Bringing to life tales of gracious sportsmanship, fierce rivalry, heartbreak and joy, it highlights the value of Sheffield's contributions and details the contributions of: Harold Wilson and Archie Robertson; Ernest Glover and William Cottrill; Ernie 'Evergreen' Harper; John and Sheila Sherwood; Sebastian Coe; and Jessica Ennis-Hill.

Scientific Approaches to Goalkeeping in Football: A practical perspective on the most unique position in sport by Andy Elleray

Do you coach goalkeepers and want to help them realise their fullest potential? Are you a goalkeeper looking to reach the top of your game? Then search no further and dive into this dedicated goalkeeping resource. Written by goalkeeping guru Andy Elleray this book offers a fresh and innovative approach to goalkeeping in football. With a particular emphasis on the development of young goalkeepers, it sheds light on training, player development, match performances, and player analysis. Utilising his own experiences Andy shows the reader various approaches, systems and exercises that will enable goalkeepers to train effectively and appropriately to bring out the very best in them.

Lightning Source UK Ltd.
Milton Keynes UK
UKOW06f1905060315

247441UK00012B/290/P